ABOUT THE AUTHOR

Erica Davies' successful career in print and digital fashion journalism spans two decades and neatly reflects the changing dynamics of media. She was one of the UK's youngest national newspaper fashion editors aged 24 at *The Sun*, a role she held for a decade before moving to *Look* magazine as fashion and beauty editor. She embraced the digital revolution by setting up her own lifestyle blog, *The Edited*, as a way of staying in touch with the industry during her first maternity leave.

She quickly grasped the power of social media and her talent for writing and styling, matched with a natural wit and warmth, made her Instagram feed a must-follow for anyone interested in fashion and interiors. Her ability to say what others are thinking and put her own unique spin on life has led to her developing a very personal connection with her hugely engaged audience. Major brands have lined up to work with Erica, leading to collections with high street names, foreign trips and numerous media appearances. Erica is married and has two children.

LEOPARD IS
A NEUTRAL

For Mum and Dad.
And, for anyone who has ever felt fashion
wasn't for them – I hope this helps.

LEOPARD IS
A NEUTRAL

A Really Useful Style Guide

ERICA DAVIES

First published in Great Britain in 2020 by Yellow Kite
An imprint of Hodder & Stoughton
An Hachette UK company

4

Copyright © Erica Davies 2020

The right of Erica Davies to be identified as the Author of the Work has
been asserted by her in accordance with the Copyright, Designs
and Patents Act 1988.

Interior illustrations © Emma Cowlam 2020

Cover artwork by Nic&Lou

A CIP catalogue record for this title is available from the British Library

Hardback ISBN 978 1 529 33371 8
eBook ISBN 978 1 529 33520 0

Typeset in Celeste by Palimpsest Book Production Limited, Falkirk, Stirlingshire

Printed and bound in Great Britain by Clays Ltd, Elcograf S.p.A.

Hodder & Stoughton policy is to use papers that are natural, renewable
and recyclable products and made from wood grown in sustainable
forests. The logging and manufacturing processes are expected to
conform to the environmental regulations of the country of origin.

Yellow Kite
Hodder & Stoughton Ltd
Carmelite House
50 Victoria Embankment
London EC4Y 0DZ

www.yellowkitebooks.co.uk

CONTENTS

FOREWORD
by Trinny Woodall

Erica and I are very similar in our missions. We want to see the light shine out of a woman's face when we've dressed her in a way that makes her feel really great about herself. It's incredibly transformative. When a woman says she feels pretty in something you've tried on her, you can help remove some of those negative messages she might have piled upon herself growing up.

As women, we want some parameters by which to make decisions.

We want to be able to refine our options – otherwise there's too *much* and it creates a paradox of choice. At which point we just walk away feeling unfulfilled.

When Susannah Constantine and I first started writing our newspaper column, then our books, they were all about saying to women, 'This is your shape, let's give you a template of things that will suit you and then go shopping'.

Women needed that message at the time because it hadn't been said before and it felt groundbreaking. Some of those rules have really stuck around today – and when I look back at those books and read them now, I can see how they may have been helpful for women to consider when dressing themselves.

However, rules are made to be broken and, over time, I have softened about the ones we wrote in those early books. So much of dressing is about creating a *feeling* – it's so important to examine how a colour or a shape makes you *feel*.

After it stopped in the UK, Susannah and I took our show abroad, where it became something much softer. And while we dressed hundreds of women who all looked very different, the emotions involved were the same. I saw women who felt lost about what they should be wearing, and I realised that they needed a more emotional response. So, if a suit wasn't quite the right shape for someone, but it was in a fantastic colour for her, that became the most important thing. I had begun to see the emotional importance of how you dress. Before, it had been a mathematical equation; now, I could appreciate it is much more about how clothes make you feel.

I met Erica when we were writing book number five, because Susannah and I had a column in *The Sun* and her team would help us on shoots for the page, dressing the women. We'd come in and have lots of different women to dress, all with different shapes. Erica quickly began to learn how I liked to look at women and we started working together, styling our books. While she brought her sense of fashion, I brought a sense of a woman's body. She taught me fashion moments too – that ability to take the high street and make it look beautiful! Especially when some things weren't quite so beautiful, she could elevate them!

There is a logic to putting clothes together. Erica talks

about 'the scan' in this book and that's exactly what I do too. Scanning is a learned art – I walk into Zara, and because I've been in that Zara so often and know where all the good things are, I can 'scan' in a couple of minutes and find those three things that are interesting. Erica and I have seen so many tops and we know at a glance which will have a bad sleeve length, for example, or whether the material is good without even touching it. When I pick up a fabric I think, 'That's great, that cut. Does it work? Will it be flattering?'

One classic rule I still obey is how to do a print clash. If you don't want to clash and are smaller on the top, pick out the paler colour in a print, while if you're bigger, pick out the darker colour. Those are basic things that still apply.

There are classic rules and then there's a layer of intuition and experience and then, on top, that emotional 'how do I feel today?' That is the *best* way to consider dressing, encouraging women to think about what makes them feel passionate in their life.

What I've always loved about Erica's style and the way she does things is that she's not a size ten, which makes her so accessible. A lot of women will use a reason like, 'My boobs are big' or, 'I don't like my bottom, so I won't do that', but when they see Erica wearing things, they think, 'Well, she's doing it'. And it inspires them to try. She lives what she breathes – and I think that's why I was drawn to her. She's always done that – even on a scrappy day in a studio, she really thought about that outfit!

You get to that point in your life where the more emotion hits you, the more you soften. I've just got to the point where

I am softer in many ways. Now though, I find there is *so* much choice out there and there are still so many women who don't know where to start. So the best thing we can do is give them inspiration to try new things – in fact, I think our responsibility with what we do is to make women feel like they can *try* different things. And I find the way Erica presents things so inspiring – from outfits, to simple posts on her Instagram stories.

That's what's so exciting about this journey on social media. It's very different from a column in a magazine. There, you're that much more removed from the reader, and it is harder to influence them to put down the article and think, 'I'm going to go into my wardrobe'. But when you are in front of them on an Instagram LIVE or a phone screen, saying, 'Do this!' or, 'Think about doing this!' your words are in their head and they'll go off and think, 'I'm going to try that today!'

However, it's so important that we also have books in our home to refer to and rely on to give us inspiration and make us think differently. I'm so happy that Erica has made the decision to write this book. You cannot read it without leaving with new ideas for yourself and your wardrobe and just feeling better about yourself.

Trinny x

Trinny Woodall, fashion expert, author and founder of Trinny London

INTRODUCTION

This may be a style guide, but it's with a *big* difference – it's a style guide without the 'rules'. It's a book for those of you who have spent years dressing with the 'shapes', 'styles' and 'colours' you've been told to by the fashion industry – and yet you still haven't nailed who you are. It's a book for those of you who want to shake out of the clothing rut you're in, or who feel 'can't' dress a certain way because of these so-called 'rules' surrounding your body shape. It's for those of you who hold back from wearing clothes that will make you happy, because you are worried about what other people might think. It's for those of you who have lost confidence in yourself and your judgement, for a variety of reasons – and who aren't sure where to go to get that back.

I'm Erica. I was a fashion editor for almost 20 years, working on the UK's biggest-selling newspapers and magazines. I helped perpetuate the myth of 'rights and wrongs' when it came to the way we should 'all' be dressing, by writing article after article about them. Until, one day, when putting something on, I felt constrained and uncomfortable – and I thought 'this doesn't make me happy'. I felt the rules were wrong; that, actually, clothes should make us happy, not feel hidden or 'less than'. They should be an extension of who we are.

And I know I'm not alone there. Now, instead of producing fashion content in print, I upload it on to my digital channels. Every day, I receive hundreds of messages from followers who want my advice and help with specific style issues – from losing their confidence after childbirth, to feeling confused about who they are and how to express that with their ward-robe; women who have spent years learning the 'rules', but still feel something is holding them back from being them-selves. I love that the ideas and suggestions I share online may have helped someone, even in a small way. Having gained so much insight from my followers, I know it's often small tweaks that can make a huge difference. That's the reason I have written this book.

A bit about me . . . I can remember proudly announcing when I was nine years old that I was going to be a journalist. Then the next time an elderly relative asked, I'd included 'fashion' into that title. I knew really early on that words and clothes were my 'thing'. I was utterly transported when I read my mum's fashion magazines – how I pored over every image and knew every name on the masthead. I wasn't sure how I'd get there, but get there I would.

And I did. During university (I read English Language at

Newcastle), I wrote to every publication asking for work experience. After university, I landed a placement within a fashion department for a morning TV show at the BBC called *Style Challenge*, where I assisted the stylists on the show, picked up clothes from press offices, made a *lot* of tea and absorbed every stylish second of it. For a girl who'd moved down to the capital city from the north-west of England, it was heaven. From there, I met the fashion editor of the *Daily Mirror*, who invited me to their offices in London's Canary Wharf for an internship. Three months led to three years. I went from sorting our returns in the fashion cupboard to compiling a style column for the weekly glossy magazine. My editor, Piers Morgan (yes, him!), made me – and my colleague Amber Graafland – the 'Store Trawlers', writing about high-street trends and photographing ourselves trying them out. Effectively, back in 2001, we did what everyone now does on Instagram!

At 24, I was made one of Fleet Street's youngest ever fashion editors when the *Sun*, the UK's biggest-selling daily newspaper, offered me that position. It was a challenge, for lots of reasons. My inherited team were my age or older. I'd only ever been an assistant, but was suddenly running a team, going into conference with the editor, coming up with a list of daily ideas and being the one who got hauled over the coals if something messed up. They say in these situations you either sink or swim – and so it seems I love a challenge!

I was there for 10 years and, in that time, transformed the fashion pages from lingerie-only, to multiple-page, trend-led photo shoots, on locations around the world using amazing photographers, models and creatives. I appeared as a fashion expert on TV and radio shows. I was the person who art-directed shoots, selected a diverse range of models, styled the clothes and, ultimately, chose the images that appeared in the newspaper. This position gave me the freedom to play around with fashion, to try out simple tricks that made a big difference – effectively learning on the job. I even met my husband there!

After taking time out to have my children, I went back to magazines – working as the fashion and beauty director on *LOOK*. It was an interesting time. I had started a fashion and lifestyle blog called *The Edited* during my second maternity leave, which kept me ticking over creatively, so I balanced writing that with the new day job, *as well as* having two very small children at home.

It was fascinating to be at *LOOK* at a time when there was a crucial shift in the print and digital worlds. Magazines – for so long heralded as the only way to receive expert advice – had to start working out how to stay relevant and stop sales from plummeting, while a surge in the numbers of people joining social media channels effectively allowed *them* to become their own online publications. It was suddenly all about digital content, meaning stylists and print journalists had to learn how to input that on top of their specialist areas. Personally, I began to be offered work because of my blog, rather than my job, which I had to turn down. My eldest was about to start primary school and I *really* wanted to be around more. Something had to give. So, I took a risk and quit, telling myself I would try to focus on working full-time for myself, whatever that might look like.

My family and I moved out of London and this gave everything a kick-start. My Instagram account had previously been a place for coffee shots and #shoefies (pictures of my shoes on the floor!), but I could now start considering it as my own kind of publication. After all, I'd been doing it for other people for almost two decades! I started documenting home renovations alongside styling ideas for this new, freelance chapter of my life. When we moved home, my account hadn't hit 10,000 followers. Four years later, there are over 150,000 – all of whom support and encourage, share and confide.

It's a surreal space, this digital arena, but it's a special one. I was named one of *The Sunday Times'* 'Top 100 Influencers' and now work in partnership with brands including Bobbi Brown, John Lewis and Omega. I have designed products for stores, including a shoe for Marks & Spencer, while a rug I featured from online retailer La Redoute become a bestseller and was renamed 'The Erica'! I have my own homeware collection – 'Edited by Erica' – for QVC, which came about because of me sharing the bold, colourful interior choices for my own home.

It's hard to determine what makes a successful online account. I think honesty and authenticity are clichéd words, but they do represent what an audience is after – particularly when the account works in a commercial capacity. I am honest about when I earn money through partnerships and whether things have been sent to me as gifts, and I always try to ask myself, 'What is this offering someone?!' every time I post a picture. I always get an *amazing* response when I talk about issues that affect us all, from body image to feeling your age. There's also a lot to be said for having a sense of humour about it all.

Instagram has levelled the playing field, allowing people from all walks of life to show off their skills, whether photographic, interiors, craft or fashion styling. I love the fact that social media has made fashion so much more democratic. I love looking at different personal style accounts, experts teaching me things; I love people asking questions or sending me messages telling me that something I have worn has inspired them. I have always loved leopard print – it's always been something of a signature – but, for me, the print encapsulates so much about personal style. This isn't a book about animal patterns, by the way – it's a catch-all title looking in a broader sense at the way you want to dress. Because whether you love it or loathe it, leopard is a print that makes a statement. It shows a confidence and self-assurance with clothing decision-making. In the general sense of this book, it's saying that you don't have to conform – you just have to hone in on the colours, prints and styles of clothes that *really* make you tick.

Your road to sartorial happiness doesn't lie in whether you have managed to track down that much-Instagrammed dress on eBay or whether you can afford to splash out on those designer shoes. Without wanting to sound trite, it goes much deeper than that. Imposter syndrome is real. If you're wearing the outfit but not *feeling* the effects, then the clothes are wearing you. It should *always* be the other way around.

Often people don't know who they really are. They feel more secure if they look like other people or wear the look that everybody says is 'in'. But women who are truly comfortable in themselves wear clothes that reflect that. It could be an amazing embellished dress, but you notice the wearer *before* the sequins. It could be a little styling quirk, like wearing a man's shirt with a maxi skirt, or a hand-me-down necklace with a sweatshirt. Feeling great in clothes is *all* about how *you* feel when you look at yourself in the mirror. Clothes off, butt naked, soul and skin bared. It has more to do with the way you deal with the reality of your own body than any gorgeous dress you could put on it. It relates to how you've been conditioned to consider your shape or your body. It is about the words your parents or carers used when they talked about you growing up or the words they used to describe others. It's the language that became commonplace when you'd talk to your friends about other people in your class at school. The words you would overhear when they put you down, versus those others used to build you up.

I want to help you unpick the negative language that has become second nature – that same language that holds you back from happiness. Those words fundamentally affect your self-esteem and the language you use internally when you look at yourself in the mirror. Those words provide the framework within which you think about your own body, your friends' bodies and also the way you perceive strangers on the train or on the Internet.

In order to feel happy in clothes, we need to feel happy with who we are beneath them. We need to make sure that the words we are using not just for ourselves, but for describing people in general, are kind. So much can be achieved with kindness – even great outfits. In sharing the words, stories and insights from nearly 20 years as a fashion editor, combined with a lifetime of feeling I was never quite *thin* or *cool* enough (which was a ridiculous waste of time, because you don't have to be anything except yourself), I hope to show you that creating a personal style that suits you, your life, your budget and your happiness is not only achievable, but opens up a whole world of confidence and possibilities.

First, though, there's a lot of stuff to sort out. Let me help with that.

Erica

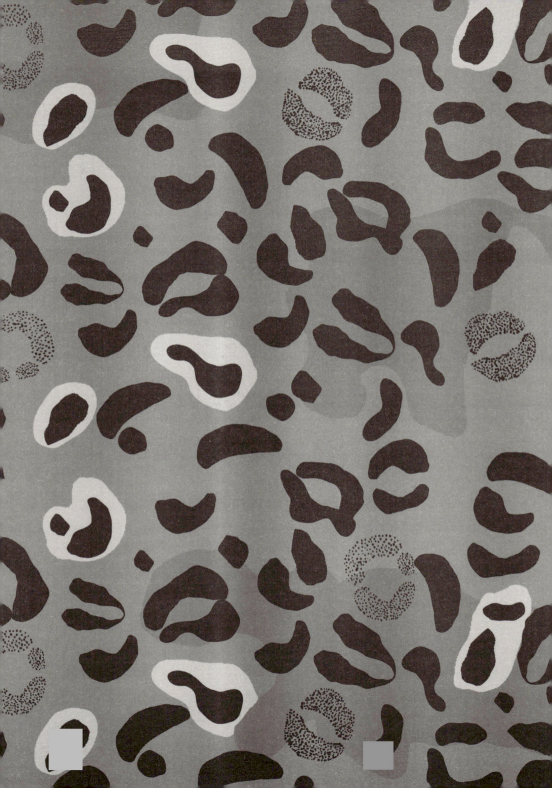

Style : Lost and Found

CHAPTER ONE

STYLE: LOST AND FOUND

When you leave your house in the morning, however you dress is the way you want the world to see you.
——Edward Enninful, Editor, British *Vogue*

It's a funny thing, style. You can feel perfectly fine in the outfits you put together for years without giving anything a second thought. Then, one day, you wake up and find you've completely lost your confidence. The 'you' who once felt fine, seems to have disappeared – and you're not sure where she's gone. While putting on an outfit has an instantly transformative effect, to empower, give confidence and create connections, it can also cause confusion. How do you know what it is you want to say with your clothes? How do you want to feel when you put them on? Who is it you want to *be*?

The fashion industry is a multi-billion-dollar global industry. It creates thousands of jobs and livelihoods – from the technology sector and garment and pattern cutting, to designers, models, moguls, journalists and digital content creators. And yet, it is often dismissed as beneath debate, as unintellectual, insignificant and, yes, a little bit shallow. People may say they're not interested in clothes, but this can often mean they don't want to *appear* as though they're interested in clothes.

Regardless of the interest, shopping is still a *huge* business for much of the world. But the way we shop has completely changed, even in the last five years. Whatever the size of a brand, it's now digital-first, with one in every five UK pounds spent online, according to a 2018 report by data and consultancy firm GlobalData. Products have to get to market *fast*, while satisfying the 'woke' customer's ever-growing demand for transparency in supply chains and product sustainability. Customers are pushing for more: more consideration from brands, more choice in sustainable garments, more pressure to buy less and buy better – and yet the fastest-growing markets are still the fast-fashion brands. Industry magazine *Retail Gazette* shared that online retailer Boohoo saw record profits of 44 per cent, thanks to its USP of recreating celebrity looks in a turnaround timeline of days, in order to sell at low prices to young customers. As a company, *Retail Gazette* says Boohoo is worth around £4 billion, more than high-street stalwart Marks & Spencer. And the magazine also shared how Inditex brands, owners of Zara and Massimo Dutti, are killing the competition in the fast-fashion arena

– their quick-turnaround, catwalk-inspired clothing earned them a revenue of £16.73 billion in 2019. This tells us that the appetite for clothes is very much there, despite the fact that, according to a Barnardo's survey, the average fashion purchase is worn just seven times.

Working across a range of national titles in the UK, I've seen first hand how many of my (often male) editors reduced style content to a few paragraphs, or scrapped an idea I'd suggested for a broader feature, replacing it instead with my team's 'verdict' on a celebrity's red-carpet outfit. And yet, here we are. A billion-pound industry, with stores now open – thanks to the Internet – 24/7. While fashion may be dismissed by some as frippery, millions of others see it as a powerful force for good. In very small ways throughout my career I have witnessed this – from messages received today on social media and time spent talking to women I've been styling in changing rooms to dressing those who have recovered from cancer, who have just given birth, who have changed gender, changed their *lives* – and I've seen how vulnerability and insecurity can disappear as soon as people feel good in their clothes.

Now my work is mainly based in the digital arena, so rather than receiving letters from readers, I get instant messages. And more than anything else I am messaged about online, requests for advice from women who feel they have lost their way – sartorially speaking – make up the majority. There's a whole host of reasons for this – everything from gaining or losing weight, to moving to another country or having a complete change of career. But more often than not, these messages are from women who have given birth, who've been in a baby bubble for nine months, who have lost a sense of non-parent, adult confidence, whose bodies have changed and who feel confused about who it is they are *now*.

Their bodies look different, their clothes don't feel right. Mentally, there's a disparity between which part of them has the most power: the mother or the other. I get it – I have two children and have been through the same thing. Twice. It's why I started my blog, 'The Edited' – I wanted a space to share outfits and style tricks that suited my body and my life right that minute. My friends and I may have become mothers, but we still wanted to know what our favourite stores were selling – and how we could find a more casual, maternity-leave style that still felt like us, despite our bodies changing a little.

It is unsettling knowing that where once you *knew* who you were, now, you don't. It's a thing; 'the mum rut' is real. Many reduce this 'rut' to a stereotype: a uniform of jeans, striped tops and Converse trainers for the entirety of their maternity leave. And, yes, there is a cliché associated with that, but so what? The familiarity of selecting comfortable pieces, each one stylish in its own simplicity, offers up a classic, unassuming, easy outfit at a time when everything around you has changed. There is something to be said for creating your own uniform – it provides comfort and fuss-free options that will always work. No experimentation required. Of course, it also signifies something much bigger than that. There has been a profound shift – and it takes a long time to adjust to this. For many, myself included, there's a real sense of keeping to ourselves how we feel about our bodies and our sense of self during this time: 'It'll be fine when I get some sleep/lose the weight'; 'No, really, I'll be fine when I *get some sleep.*' It's a 'this too shall pass' mentality that just adds pressure during a period when, actually, there's a lot of fairly heavy stuff going on (hello baby!).

But remember you're not alone. There are millions going through the exact same thing and there has been a very bold shift in the parenting paradigm since I gave birth in 2010. It's not even that long ago, but *so much* has changed. Where previously we shared the process with friends or learned tips from magazine articles and books, now parenting is a hugely popular social media category: '*sharenting*'.

While there are thousands online who portray a realistic, comforting view of the first few months of motherhood, I will be honest and say that I am grateful that Instagram wasn't as prevalent when I first became a mother. There are *so many* moot points. Issues about whether you share photos of your baby online to begin with, or show them, but disguise their face. Whether you accept commercial relationships with brands *because* you share images of your child, which could lead to potential parent-shaming within comments, direct messages or even on anonymous gossip forums, where people go to criticise those they've never met because of their crime in sharing their lives on the Internet.

While I spent the first six months in pyjamas, with no make-up and a return to my natural colour (because I thought going dark would be easier than my usual blonde), now there's a pressure for people to look great immediately, share tastefully art-directed first images of baby, then get back on to their account looking incredible, posing next to their cashmere-clad baby, brand-new buggy, all smiles, wearing four-inch heels and all-white ensembles. I'm joking, of course, but I can only imagine how 'perfect' images, outfits and lifestyles played out digitally, available 24/7, could affect a vulnerable mindset. That feeling that you're doing it all 'wrong', looking 'wrong', while feeling envious and unsettled seeing other people at a similar stage of life seemingly coping perfectly, is overwhelming. Combine all that with a lack of sleep and it's a potent brew for unhappiness.

For those who have experienced, or are stuck in a 'rut', it's often difficult to analyse whether it's a reaction to our sense of self, a lifestyle change, a response to a change in our bodies – or just being really fed up of your own wardrobe! It's not just restricted to childbirth, of course; it can also happen if you've gained or lost weight, for example. Where once you knew the contours and had a sense of your own body, it might suddenly feel a little alien. And where on earth do you start when you feel like that? It can happen if you're completely changing careers, or even if you're going back to a different working environment after a job break.

Developing a style that tells people who you are before you even open your mouth sounds like a big ask, particularly if you are currently feeling oddly separate from your previous self. But, actually, if you find a few nailed-down casual looks that make you feel confident enough to be your true self, that's all you need. So perhaps the idea of the jeans, striped top and trainers isn't so much of a rut as an outfit superhero. Think of these pieces as an entry point to further developing your personal style.

WHAT *IS* PERSONAL STYLE?

As I mentioned, style is something often downplayed as fashion frippery, but clothes have the ability to make us feel *really good*. It's why, according to the British Council, fashion is a business worth approximately £26 billion and creates around 800,000 jobs. A decade ago, we might have spent hours browsing the high street, or stuck to our preferred brands to give ourselves an easy life. Now, we're just as likely to browse and shop on our way to work via our smartphones, which give us instant access to the looks and recommendations of people we follow on social media (swipe up and buy!) or friends, all around the world. In fact, research by GlobalData suggests, mobiles will account for over 40 per cent of online expenditure by 2024 (around £33 billion of spending power). It has made us much more open to trying new brands, but also much more impatient about getting the styles we want *right now*.

But while some women seem to be able to get it all together, go to the gym at 6am, dress their children in ironed, toothpaste-free school uniforms, make a healthy, nutritious breakfast, put on their own crisp white shirt, pair it with that perfect camel coat, get themselves out of the door on time *and* nail their signature pillar-box red lipstick by 8am, many of us get by and make do, without ever really knowing which style it is we really *like*.

For me, my personal style is something that's just *there*, formed over many years from a collection of 'yes, no and maybe I'll try it' conversations in my head as I went shopping. You know how, when people talk about, for example, wedding dress shopping and 'they' always say the first dress you try on is usually 'the one'? Well, when I go shopping, either online or in a shop, it's generally the first couple of pieces that immediately speak to me that I end up buying. More than current trends, it's always been about how my clothes make me feel and whether they suit me. Over time I've worked out exactly what I like. I know the colours and shapes I love and the pieces that suit my curvy-bottomed shape. I am instinctively attracted to the pieces that I know will work for me and I can scan and edit shop floors quickly (I'm going to share how I do this in Chapter Six). And when I say 'work', I mean those items that I know I will feel comfortable and happy wearing – for *me*, no one else. It's a honed skill, developed over many years of doing it professionally for other people as well as myself. But what *is* personal style?

Firstly, there is a real difference between style and taste. Taste is the pieces you select, while style is the way in which you put your taste together. A person with their own sense of style has a strong look or aesthetic that may not necessarily adhere to convention in the same way as taste. It's the exterior package-deal response to the life you lead – the places you've travelled to, the inspiration you've had, the books you've read. There's nothing judgemental about 'style'. Many think it's about fashion trends, but style is more fluid and way more individual than that. One person's style might have its foundation in a cultural or religious dress code, but with a twist that makes it uniquely theirs. Style is individuality, about being able to put pieces together in a way that suits the wearer's personality, so they look comfortable and happy wearing them. When your wardrobe is a collection of all your favourite things, they will make a statement about who you are. There's something really satisfying about knowing that when you can look at them all, hanging up, you can say, 'That's me.' You can express yourself honestly and with confidence.

The great thing about developing your personal style is that you don't have to dress the same every day. It can be a slightly different version of you, depending on what you need to do that day – with a sprinkle of something consistently you, whether that's a bag, or a shoe shape, or just a simple accessory or lip colour. And it's ever-evolving. I still take inspiration from everywhere. In my mind, I have hundreds of virtual scrapbooks of looks floating around: style icons whose outfits have inspired me; fashion editors in magazines who have created amazing shoots; and characters on TV shows who have inspired me to rummage around vintage shops. Now there's even *more* inspiration to take in; from Instagram and Pinterest, to blogs and Tumblr, people show off their personal style on every platform. According to influencer marketing agency Takumi, Instagram is considered the most influential – where 68 per cent of 18–24-year-olds interviewed said they would be more likely to buy after seeing an item on someone they follow.

And while *of course* it's OK to take inspiration from celebrities and influencers, clothes create your own identity and form of personal self-expression, so it's important to make sure that you're wearing the clothes that feel right on you, rather than creating a facsimile of someone else's outfit. Your own interpretation is what makes 'personal' style real, relatable, but also unique. I would describe it a bit like taking all the different elements of your personality – the office you, the casual you, the mother you, the wife/partner you, the you who likes dressing with a masculine twist, the you who sometimes likes being a bit sexy, the girly you – then mixing them all together in garment form. I'm happiest in pieces with a bohemian touch and feminine whimsy. I'm unapologetic about print and colour, but equally happy occasionally wearing dark colours. I like high necks and longer hemlines. I love vintage coats and statement bags. I would like to think that my style tells people who I am before I even open my mouth.

An open, honest mind is crucial when it comes to trying to pinpoint what you want to wear (and say with your clothes). Don't take your taste for granted – ask yourself *why* you like certain pieces or mixing certain things together. Below are some questions for you to answer about your feelings towards your own style. Grab a pencil and see what you come up with:

• What do you reach for time and again that helps you feel more 'you'? Dresses
• Why, on some days, do you want to add a pair of earrings or a necklace, while on other occasions you don't? Do they make you feel good on some days and less so on others?
• Are there days when you want to stand out, and others when you'd rather blend in? Yes, it depends
• Would you steer clear of certain colours on the days when you feel less confident? No
• What are your happy colours – the colours you would wear if you felt really confident? Bright colors
• Do you ever take note of when something makes you feel good or happy? Can you say why that is? Yes, the way it makes me feel. I wear it over again

- The same goes for when something doesn't. Can you think about occasions when you don't feel so good in something? *If something is too tight or doesn't feel right.*

It's important to think about what doesn't suit you or make you feel good, but don't allow that negativity to outweigh the feeling when you wear something that lifts your spirits. We listen to the negative stuff way too much – and that can often stifle any positives. Question the little voice inside your head that tells you something looks great on another person, but that you could 'never pull it off'. Why couldn't you? Have you tried it? We need to get to a place where clothes make us feel positive. Paying attention to the pieces you reach for or are attracted to and asking yourself 'Why?' more often helps you learn so much more about yourself. Ask yourself what really makes you feel joyful when you think about colours and fabrics and shapes. Start there.

RECONSIDER 'THE RULES'

During my teen years, I always worried that boys wouldn't like me if I didn't wear clothes that showed off my shape, but, deep down, that thought made me feel uncomfortable. For many reasons, but mainly as an adult now thinking about this, it makes me sad that I thought I needed that validation. Many of us are similarly conditioned by other people's reactions to our clothing choices. How many times have you heard comments like, 'You can't wear that' or 'That really doesn't suit you' or even 'You're the wrong shape for that'? These comments may come from a place of good intention, but the mixture of embarrassment, upset and awkwardness resulting from others' perceptions of how we look can stay with us into adulthood and beyond. Have you ever been put off buying a certain item of clothing because a magazine article told you that you were the 'wrong' shape? Or watched a TV fashion show that suggested you should 'never' wear a particular style of trousers if you are a certain size? It might make us want to experiment less with our style, stay 'safe' and inoffensive. Often, we can hold on to these societal expectations forever: 'You're too pale for that colour', 'Don't wear stripes if you want to look thin – you don't have the hips for them', 'You're blonde, you can't wear yellow' . . . There are probably dozens of 'rules' you have processed from childhood that have formed how you consider your own sense of self and the pieces you're 'allowed' to wear, even decades later. Here are some off the top of my head:

1. 'Those stripes make you look even wider.'
2. 'You're short; you can't wear a midi skirt.'
3. 'Tall women shouldn't wear heels. You shouldn't be taller than your partner.'
4. 'You shouldn't have long hair in your forties.'
5. 'You don't look good in those jeans; your bum is too big.'
6. 'You really don't have the legs for miniskirts.'
7. 'You're wearing too much make-up.'
8. 'You're too big to wear a bikini.'
9. 'Don't wear tights with open-toed shoes, it looks awful.'
10. 'At your age, you can't wear . . . '

This is *exactly* the kind of advice we've all grown up with – so much so, that it's become second nature; it's simply what has *always* been written. It's the way women have historically been spoken to. It's the way we, ourselves, speak about other women. It's the way we have been taught to assess and judge ourselves, our female relatives and our friends. It's the way we have been taught to dress, because, duh, those are 'the rules'. And here's the thing: we have accepted them. Never questioned them. In order to get dressed, look presentable and get out of the house in the morning, these rules must be obeyed. And God help anyone who hasn't – for she will be judged for that!

How odd it is to assume women come in a one-size-fits-all. All of us, perfectly packaged, in a few distinct and limited body shapes – where the same instructions on dressing suit each person of each shape. Fundamentally, many of these style 'rules' perpetuated a myth that in order to look good, we had to shrink or disguise ourselves. We had to pretend that we didn't have any flaws, fat, hips, boobs or, hell, any other kind of body that didn't conform to a historic, male-imposed definition of feminine perfection. We were told that our outfits should be cleverly constructed to fool the eye of any onlookers, lest our body 'issues' be obvious: 'Never wear ankle straps on shoes because they make your legs look short – and they draw attention to a cankle (a calf + ankle)'; 'You can *never* wear a mini dress *and* "show off" your cleavage, because that's just *too much*.' But if you want to take attention away from your body, you *can* show off your cleavage because that will draw the eye upwards, towards your face, which means no one will look at your body.

For a *long* time, fashion magazines have spoken to women in that patronising, old-fashioned way too. What are the 'must-have' items, what are this season's style do's and don'ts, alongside those (truly awful) 'who wore it best' articles – pitting women against each other based solely on what they wear. In fact, for a long time *I* was the one writing those articles and perpetuating those myths. As a fashion editor, I wrote cover lines to lure the reader in with the 'must-haves' and the 'trends you simply need to have right now'. I produced page after page of features showing the 'best' styles to wear to 'suit' your body shape. I discussed how curves should *never* wear a horizontal stripe. How shapeless garments will drown you, but you shouldn't wear a waist belt if you're plus size – you need to wear pieces that 'nip you in' at the waist and 'flatter' your hips. Why you should never go sleeveless if you're bigger than a size 16.

What I know is this: articles like that – including all those I wrote – only serve to tell us that who we are isn't good enough. The words feed that internal voice telling us that we aren't enough as we are – that we *need* more, that we need to *be* more. Can you think of any men's magazine fashion pages which dictate how they should 'cover up' a belly, 'elongate' short legs or 'disguise' a narrow shoulder? Exactly.

As a teenager, I remember avidly poring over pages to analyse the jeans I 'should' wear as a 'pear shape'. I remember holding tight the notion that as a curvy size 12, horizontal stripes were not my friend. As I headed out on a Saturday, shopping with my babysitting earnings, I eschewed black because I'd read that as a sallow-skinned, brown-eyed brunette, I should never wear it. I never went for horizontal stripes, unless the stripes thinned around the waist to give the illusion of a smaller shape. Blue and green should *never* be seen.

These 'rules' were filed away neatly in my brain for years as 'fact', constantly being brought to the fore when scanning a store – even as someone who worked in the industry. I'm not sure which part of the style rule indoctrination broke me first, but the little voice in my head telling me it was all bunkum became louder and louder over time. Until, finally, I reached the 'Why *can't* I wear this, if I *like* it and it feels *good?*' stage. I have a *whole* chapter on deciphering these so-called rules later in the book (Chapter Seven), because I have a *lot* to say about them.

My personal style evolution has been gradual. Historically, I'm the type of person who would look to what others were wearing in certain situations, absorb my surroundings, then try to find ways to reinterpret them in my own way. In my twenties, there were loads of trends I forced on myself because I thought that's what everyone did. I wore skinny jeans, even though – with my curvy bum – I felt self-conscious wearing them. I wore a lot of black, because I considered that's what 'people in fashion' did, even though I was happiest in colour. I spent huge amounts of money on expensive, high-heeled boots that I could barely walk in! It all left me feeling a bit like I had disappeared. Right now, in my forties, I think my personal style is something my younger self could definitely get on board with. I'm more in tune with the way my personality and body want to wear clothes.

Social media would have us believe that other people have a confidence that we don't possess; that others can share their outfits and their bodies in a way that we cannot imagine. But, really, clothes are just clothes. One day you might want to wear something sparkly to the supermarket, while another day you might try on a trouser suit for a day out with a friend. If those pieces make you feel uncomfortable, you never have to wear them again. But if, on the other hand, you feel like a goddess, or just really, really happy, maybe they are things that you should repeat. The more you try these little things, the easier it will become. And remember too, that they really can just be little things.

Basic separates that can help create your outfit superheroes
Making sure your wardrobe has a few key pieces that will make you feel fantastic, comfortable *and* stylish whenever you reach for them, will make a huge difference to getting dressed. Consider them your own personal superheroes – wearing just one will give you a secret style boost – but they're also the perfect mixers to start having fun creating outfits. Here are some examples of mine:

- Cashmere/merino wool crew neck in useful, easy-to-mix-with-other-things shades, such as navy, camel, maroon, khaki, cream and grey.
- Thick cotton blue-and-white striped long-sleeved tee.
- Thin cotton printed turtleneck (for prints, think spots, stripes, leopard, florals) for layering.
- Boyfriend-shape khaki chinos.
- Navy or black wide-leg trousers in a flimsy fabric that could be worn under dresses or with a jumper.
- Leopard or zebra print pull-on midi skirt.
- Khaki shacket (shirt/jacket), utility/army style.
- White leather plimsolls.
- Chunky lace-up black ankle boots.
- Animal print or metallic leather flat shoes (ballet shoe style).

Add trends to your personal style in small details, rather than committing to entire looks. Stick to your gut and you won't go far wrong – great life advice generally, but definitely with clothes.

FIVE POINTS TO TAKE AWAY

1. Don't hold on to the archaic 'rules' you were told as a child. You can create your *own* style rules.

2. Take inspiration from everywhere – then start to work out what you like about it.

3. You do not need to listen to other people's opinions about your body *or* your outfit.

4. Clothes can be energy-changing superheroes; it's about finding the pieces that make *you* feel invincible.

5. Learn to listen to yourself.

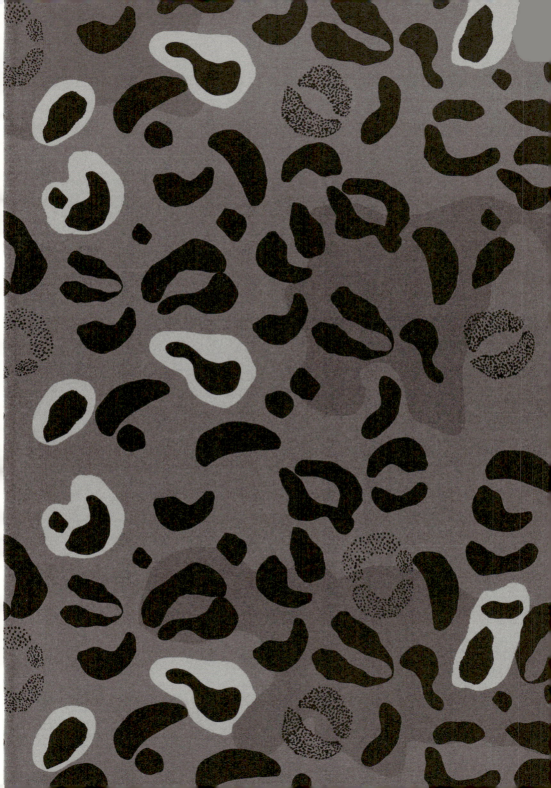

The Naked Truth

CHAPTER TWO

THE NAKED TRUTH

*Fashion is what you're offered four times a year by
designers. And style is what you choose.*

—Lauren Hutton

As women, we are constantly being sold to. We are at the
perfect crossroads of capitalism – we are told to *buy* things
in order to look a certain way – and patriarchy, where women
have always been physically held to account, based on the
judgements of male society. In order to look how we are
supposed to, we're told to buy *more*, while popping in for
regular threading, waxing, bleaching and replenishing a phar-
macy-sized toiletries cabinet in order to make ourselves look
better. And yet, there has been a subtle shift in parameters.

Beauty treatments are now described as 'self-care', in an
attempt to make them sound slightly more progressive and
less about 'vanity'. There's even a new vocabulary of weight
loss, where glossy magazine cover lines don't attempt to lure
you in with their promise of a '10-lb drop' or instructions on
'how to control your eating'. Now, they're all about teaching

us how to 'get strong' or 'be a healthier you'. 'Wellness' is an extremely lucrative industry, but are we just gift-wrapping the same demands made upon women in a shiny new way? Social media, while still showcasing so much of the 'perfection selling', has also been a drum-banger for inclusivity, where body positivity – a practice of valuing women's beauty at every size, shape and physical ability – is long overdue and *definitely* positive. But I wonder whether it's all just white noise. Are we listening and taking in the notion that beauty comes in many packages or are we paying it lip service, while still silently judging others *and* ourselves for not living up to the long-held societal standards of female beauty, regardless of that shift in parameters?

There have been a *lot* of changes and there is a *lot* of noise. Trying to square a constantly updating 'woke' world with a little bit of brain space to process it all is exhausting – and can leave you wondering who it is you *actually* are. Consider this as a sartorial example: as a magazine editor, my working week office wardrobe was sorted with a mix of dresses and smart separates, usually with a bold lipstick and statement jewellery. Yet at the weekend I was totally and utterly lost. I had a self-imposed rule that jeans didn't suit my curvy thighs, so casual clothes were an enigma. What on *earth* do you wear if you *don't* wear jeans? Then after giving birth, my body shape changed again, but because I hadn't got to grips with clothes to suit my casual new chapter, I had absolutely no idea what I should be wearing while on maternity leave.

My working wardrobe armour was off and I felt exposed and vulnerable – and without the self-esteem boost of my day-to-day office job, I had no clue who I was anymore. Rock bottom happened one day after my husband suggested we leave our baby with my mum for a couple of hours so he could take me out for dinner. I remember standing in front of my wardrobe sobbing, because dress after dress looked 'awful' (the word I used) on my stretched and 'flabby' (I'd probably say 'disgusting' or 'fat', to be honest) post-baby body. Now, I can see this was less about the clothes and more about how I felt about myself, right there, standing in that bedroom. The reality was that I was incredibly lucky: I had just had a beautiful, healthy baby, I had a partner who loved me and my supportive mum was sitting downstairs helping us out. But I'd lost sight of who I was and blaming my stretched, post-baby body for my wardrobe and entire world being 'terrible' was easier than looking for any answers.

Let me stress the point: body image has such a *huge* impact on the clothes we wear that we can only get to a happy place when we resolve those issues. A little while ago I wrote an Instagram caption while on holiday about wearing my first bikini in nine years (the first time since having my eldest child). I had wavered about putting it on that morning, but then just thought, 'Sod it! Why do I feel so ashamed about my own body?' As I typed away on my phone, lying next to the ocean, feeling the warmth of the Greek sun on my face, the words flowed . . . because I suddenly felt free. It was as though acknowledging how I felt about wearing a swimsuit in public released years of feeling 'bad' about myself. The shame of not looking 'like the models look' disappeared, because I'd said it out loud.

For as long as I can remember I had 'apologised' for my body, by covering up in hard-to-get-on swimsuits. I would immediately reach for a kaftan if I was going to walk around a swimming pool or on a beach, lest the holidays of the poor folks on the sunloungers next to mine were ruined as they caught sight of my thighs. I wrote about how, when we all lie there worrying about people passing silent judgements on our bodies, the reality is that they're *not* – they are all too busy worrying about their own. And, actually, *who the hell cares*? We all deserve to feel that sun on our skin as much as the next person.

It was my most liked social media post to date. Sharing those feelings of vulnerability combined with a 'F*ck it! Who cares?' attitude struck a chord – and even to this day I receive messages from women telling me they've just worn a bikini for the first time in years. Of course, it takes time to get to a place where we feel that sense of confidence and to care less about the opinions of strangers. It takes strength to accept yourself as you are right now, rather than thinking your life will be complete and wonderful once you've lost a bit of weight, or gained a few pounds, or found a partner, or a new job. It really won't. But finding a clothing style that makes you feel genuinely comfortable and happy, as the person you are right now, definitely will.

It's the same feeling I had when I returned to work after giving birth. I felt so utterly conflicted about who it was I was supposed to be. It was fine at home: I'd reduced my hours to three days a week and my son was being looked after by his grandparents for the rest of the time, but something inside had changed and I *knew* I was a different person. It wasn't even just the physical changes – although they were *so* difficult to navigate. I'd put weight on during my pregnancy and then very much enjoyed the cake and coffee aspect of my maternity leave! The work clothes that had once made me feel powerful, just felt wrong. I'd been out of office action for an entire year and totally lost my confidence. I was one of only a few mothers on the team and I was terrified of allowing that fact to control the narrative. 'Of *course* I can stay late', 'Yes I'll be at that meeting' I would say, all the while desperately tapping away on my phone under the desk, trying to organise alternative childcare arrangements. Where before my role had defined me as a person, now I was conflicted. How would I possibly be any good at my job when I wasn't really sure who I was anymore? And I just didn't know what I should wear to try to replace those parts of my personality that had ebbed away when I gave birth.

I'm sure many of us can relate to the issue of returning to the workplace after a significant chunk of time off, particularly after having children. Who on earth are we? What can we possibly contribute to this business? And what the hell should I be wearing now? In the end, I took the emotion out of it. I accepted that I had changed, that my body had changed and I needed to reboot, take stock and understand my new body. I built my sartorial confidence back up slowly, focusing on simple block colour uniform dressing: dress + ankle boots + statement necklace, or blazer + crew-neck jumper + wide-leg trousers + statement earrings. I searched on auction sites for pre-loved Marni necklaces and bought a second-hand Anya Hindmarch bag. They were simple things, but they gave me a little nudge in the right direction towards getting back into my stride.

CUTTING THE WORK OUT OF OFFICE DRESSING

One of the many things I love about social media is the accessibility to people; being able to message directly, particularly if you want to ask someone a question or advice. I receive hundreds of messages per day, with most being about the same sorts of dressing issues. It's one of the reasons I started a regular series within my Instagram stories, called 'Sunday Styling', where I look at specific fashion trends and show how I would wear them, or themes, including workwear or jeans alternatives. Office wear is one of the main subjects I'm regularly asked for advice about, specifically from women who are stuck in a work-related style rut or those who are about to return to work after having a baby. Whether it relates to dressing to suit a formal office situation or one with more dress code flexibility, or simply addressing changes in body shape and confidence, the working wardrobe can be an emotional minefield. But it doesn't have to be – let me try to help.

If you don't need to be suited and booted for the office, it makes sense for your everyday wardrobe to work harder and be less compartmentalised. But when was the last time you really looked at your own work wardrobe? Are you going through the formal office dress code motions, with room to add a bit more 'you' into the mix? Or have you had a career break after children and are worried about what will work now your body and life have totally changed? Today, by the very nature of women's fashion, there is way more choice of clothing out there. The trends governing what we can or should wear keep changing, so it's not always as simple as having a 'uniform' – either an actual uniform or a simple tee and jeans capsule version. Mostly, men just need to wear a suit and perhaps change their tie, whereas for women there are a myriad issues: tights or no tights, heels or flats, too short, too loose, too long and what our colleagues and boss might deem 'work-appropriate'. I wonder whether a lot of professional identity is not only based on how you perform, but also about the clothes you wear. You don't want to stand out for being too bold, but you don't want to blend in and get lost either. And you definitely want to show your style. But stylish doesn't need to be loud and in-your-face at work. It really doesn't need to shout and scream to command attention. Stylish is just as much about holding your own in a meeting as it is about being dressed comfortably and confidently.

If you're returning to work after having a baby, there will probably be a lot of emotional baggage coming along with you on your commute back to the office. If you're anything like I was, it's in a big mixed bag filled with guilt for leaving the confines of your baby bubble, a quiet excitement at the prospect of adult company and hot coffee *and* feeling a bit out of sorts with your body. Please don't make yourself feel bad for putting on weight and not losing it *immediately*. It happens – you're not alone there! What it *will* take is time, trying to reconcile the two parts of your life – the mum-you and the work-you – particularly if it's your first child and you have never experienced your office life as a mother before. It's a tricky transition, but try to reframe your return to work in a different way. You *are* a completely different person now and that gives you an opportunity to change things up style-wise. Don't feel you have to self-consciously cover up or wear baggy clothes that make you feel awkward and uncomfortable, just because you're a size or two bigger than you may have been before you left to go on maternity leave. Rather than hiding yourself under your clothes, you can use your return to make bold new choices with shapes and colours you may not have worn before.

Pay no attention to the dress size you 'should' be or 'once were' and use comfort as your guide. No one will see the label and it really doesn't matter. The most important thing is to regain your confidence. Perhaps choose a dress that skims, rather than clings to your body, or a pair of high-waisted, wide-leg trousers worn with a double-breasted blazer and a crew-neck jumper. A knitted coordinated skirt and jumper set worn with knee-high boots might be a comfortable and practical addition to your office wardrobe. Look at the pieces that already make you feel comfortable and base outfits around them – whether that's a pair of black trousers or a Breton top. You might still be breastfeeding, so need to express at work. If so, consider layering a cotton camisole under a button-up blouse, or look to shirt dresses that will allow easy access when you need it. Keep things simple at first and regain your confidence slowly. It may be that you just want to wear black for your first month – and that's absolutely fine, you could always add a bold lipstick or a statement shoe as well to lift it and make the style truly yours. If there is one thing I keep repeating in this book, it's to be kind to yourself. Do things in your own way and at your own pace.

A big factor in the world of workwear is in your choice of fabric. The better a fabric hangs, the better the silhouette, the better your posture will be and therefore the more confident you will feel. For example, a silk mix shirt under a suit jacket or blazer will move and feel much better than a fitted cotton shirt, which might make you feel a bit 'stiff' and restricted. It will also add a feminine twist to a more masculine corporate look. You could even try adding a black ribbon around the collar as a little styling quirk. A blouse with blouson sleeves, a ruffle around the neckline or even an oversized collar will all update a classic pair of trousers or a skirt. You could even play around with your style and layer a blouse beneath a pinafore dress, or under a plain crew-neck jumper, paired with a bottom half of your choosing.

Think about colour and tones – rather than plain black, how about a pair of charcoal-grey wide-leg trousers worn with a dove-grey blouse and grey check blazer? Try adding a vintage belt or a pair of statement earrings – accessories that will add personality. Add a structured tote bag and layer a complementary-coloured overcoat on top of the whole look (I will look at colour-mixing further in Chapter Three) – a dusty pink or sage-green would work beautifully with the grey palette. Push out of those office-appropriate colour combinations and try separates in modern tones. A pair of sky-blue trousers teamed with white, muted shades of lilac and grey, khaki and sage green, or a mix of white, cream and camel. You could consider wearing a tailored leather jacket with cropped trousers in two complementary colours, such as navy blue and black, rather than a one-colour traditional trouser suit. If you like the idea of cropped trousers, but aren't sure about the shoes to wear with them, don't worry. I would suggest that black fabric boots with a small heel will always look smart, because the top of the boot will 'hide' under the hemline of the trousers and won't break up the look with straps or flashes of ankle! You could also try wearing opaque tights under your trousers with a lace-up brogue, or wear with classic court shoes, in the same colour as the trousers.

Look at the pieces you wear a lot *out* of the office – so if you're a skirt + tee shirt + flat shoe wearer, try elevating your fabric choices and recreate that particular equation for work. For example, try a textured black below-the-knee skirt (perhaps leather), worn with a smarter silk-mix tee shirt, underneath a printed or contrast-coloured jacket and a pair of black patent flats. If you love wearing a jumpsuit off-duty, how about trying a smarter one for work? A long-sleeved, wide-leg jumpsuit that you could wear with comfortably-heeled court shoes and a jacket is a chic and easy way to get dressed for the office. Wearing something like a jump-suit or a dress takes a lot of the stress out of getting ready in the morning, as it's just one item that requires little to no extra styling, particularly if it already feels as though you've done a day's work before 9am! In the winter, try layering a thin polo neck or long-sleeved tee shirt under-neath a short-sleeved jumpsuit – with a sleeveless jacket over the top.

Tailored separates that will mix and match in lots of ways will not only give you multiple outfit combinations both in and out of work, but also the opportunity to add a bit of yourself in there too. Jewellery is an easy way to do this – for example, a vintage pair of gold hoop earrings, or a sentimental family piece that will make you feel special and give you a little boost of inner confidence. Look on pre-loved auction sites, such as eBay or Vestiaire Collective, for designer classics such as a Burberry trench or a Mulberry tote bag that will help give your workwear a bit of personality. By focusing on the small at first, the big can come later. Don't try to do everything all at once.

YOUR FASHION MINDSET

As a fashion editor, I styled lots of women (and some men) for their 'after' shots for fitness and diet pages. It was an exercise in the psychology of self and of style. Just as a hair-dresser gets all the gossip from a client, a stylist is often the person to whom people reveal their insecurities. As the only other person in the room as they dressed, I would get warts-and-all access to their anxieties. It was, understandably, emotional. There would be admissions that they hadn't looked at themselves properly in the mirror for years, preferring to ignore what they weren't happy with. Confessions that they hadn't wanted to be intimate with their partners because of their body hang-ups or, worse, that their partners had left after they'd lost a bit of weight and shown a new-found confidence.

Dressing other people is a delicate balancing act between curator and counsellor. While a model is paid to wear the clothes a stylist chooses, for something like a 'makeover' there needs to be a huge element of trust. Trust that the stylist won't make them feel 'less than' while they're standing in their underwear – and a trust that the clothes selected will help create a look that suits, flatters and helps build up inner confidence. Sometimes it takes another person to help you see yourself in a new light. I hope that's what this book will do for you.

But there are simple tricks that help move this process along. Doing something as simple as standing and looking at yourself in a full-length mirror, while only wearing your pants, goes a long way to unpacking the feelings you're harbouring towards your body. Try to look at yourself as a stylist would: without criticism, without the need for disgust or pain – just assess which clothes will work. Try to take out the emotion of being 'yourself' entirely and look pragmatically at who you are. This may be a big leap for some of us. It may be that you haven't really looked at yourself properly for years, but it's important. You may look at yourself and see flaw after flaw, but you're the only one. Everyone else sees the beauty of you (and if they don't, they're not worth your time!). It's an amazing thing – your body – so maybe it's time to start appreciating it for where it's got you so far.

Where did you put that pencil? Ask yourself these questions:

- What do you see when you look at yourself? Answer *only* with positive words.
- Say out loud what you like about your body.
- What makes you proud about your body?
- Describe which parts of your body you are happy to show in your clothes.
- Think about why you are happy to show these parts.

Think about specific items of clothing:

- Where would you be happy and comfortable with the hemline of a skirt or dress sitting? What is your perfect happy length?
- How does a mini make you feel?
- How does a maxi make you feel?
- How does a midi make you feel?
- What about sleeve lengths? What length makes you feel most comfortable?
- Would you wear a strappy top on its own? Ask yourself why. If not, would you consider layering it

over a longer-sleeved top? Or underneath a blazer?
Think about ways it could be styled without it 'just'
being a strappy top.

- Are you happy to wear necklines that show a bit of
  cleavage? Ask yourself why.
- Do you like yourself in high necklines?

Talk to yourself about trousers:

- Do you like wearing them?
- Do you wear jeans? Do you wear them because
  everyone else does or because they make you happy?
- What shape of trouser makes you feel most
  comfortable?
- Are you happy in more fitted styles or wider leg?

Tell yourself again what you like about your body. Repeat
often.

Forget all the rules you were taught. You only get one
body and one life – stop living it by apologising for who you
are. Once you start to like yourself, you can get a clearer
vision of who it is you want to be. And creating your individual style starts right there.

FIVE POINTS TO TAKE AWAY

1. It takes strength, but accepting yourself as you are *right now* is so important.

2. Take a pragmatic look at yourself in your underwear and try to take the emotion out of getting dressed.

3. Think about the pieces that make you feel most yourself when you put them on.

4. Focus on small changes at first – big ones can come later.

5. Your body is an incredible thing. Never feel you have to hide it away.

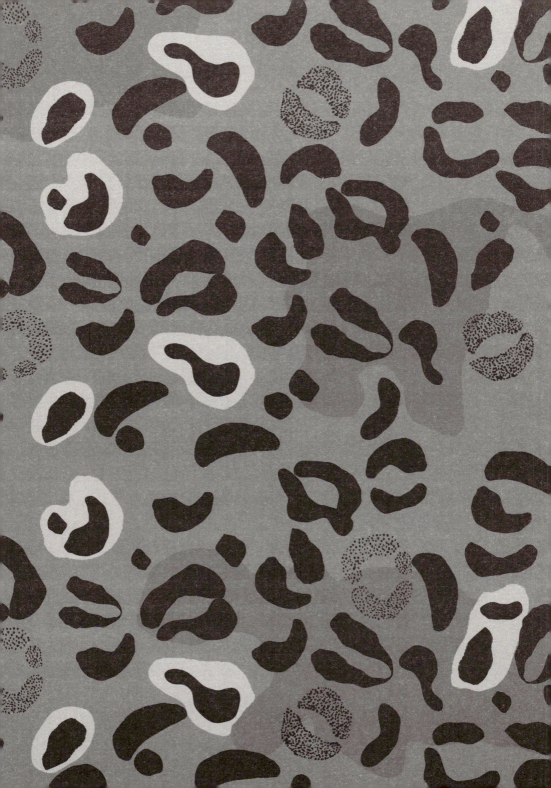

Rediscover Your Wardrobe Gems

CHAPTER THREE

REDISCOVER YOUR WARDROBE GEMS

Style is the only thing you can't buy. It's not in a shopping bag, a label or a price tag. It's something reflected from our soul to the outside world – an emotion.

—Alber Elbaz

Imagine opening up your wardrobe in the morning and not feeling overwhelmed. Imagine it filled with pieces that serve a positive purpose, clothes that make you feel happy, that you know will really work for you, as well as with each other, and that will allow getting dressed to be a pleasure, not a chore. This is what I want to help you create. First things first, you need to get ready to be wardrobe-focused and ruthless. You need to assess what it is you're attracted to, and you need to be truthful in this appraisal and with what currently fits. Anything that is there as a 'One day this will fit me' purchase or a 'This used to fit me' buy needs to be honestly evaluated. These are the things that eat away at your soul to punish you. Over the top? I don't think so. Think about it. Every item you still own that no longer does up, or that you loved once upon a time, but that doesn't really have a place in this current chapter of your life, serves as a daily crap suggestion to yourself that you can always 'be better'.

You're a size 14, but you've still got that size 10 skirt hanging there – no longer worn, but you keep it because it reminds you of that time when you worked in an office, went out four times a week and drank mojitos.

This tangible reminder isn't doing you any good. It's neither useful nor helpful to hold on to it, because you don't *need* that skirt any more. It hangs there and taunts you to be 'that' version of you, because the current one isn't good enough. This 'you' doesn't get a chance to get to the bottom of a hot mug of coffee, let alone a bottomless jug of cocktails. Hold on to the actual memories and ditch the physical reminder. Enough of that kind of thinking – you are good enough, *right now*.

THE RAIL OF TRUTH

We need an honest wardrobe review. For this we need three things: time, a full-length mirror and a rail. Go and buy yourself a rail – a cheap one will do (or you could splash out and go for something that will fit in beautifully with the aesthetics of your bedroom or living space!). Regardless, get that rail up. If your flat or house doesn't have room for a rail, consider other options such as a picture rail, door frame, cupboard or around the top of a wardrobe – basically anywhere that allows you to hang up your clothes. Before we get to the serious business of total overhaul, let's try an experiment.

Place everything you wear during the month on that rail (or picture rail!). You can go back to the rail on a daily basis if you want to wear the same jeans or jumper or scarf, but every single item you wear over that four-week period needs to be hung up on the rail. You will very quickly realise that the items you reach for time and again are the building blocks of your wardrobe. They're your wardrobe superheroes, your go-tos, your sartorial safety net. They need to be kept because you will be able to use them as the basis for all your other outfits.

After your month is over, take everything – and I mean everything – that is left *in* your wardrobe, out of your wardrobe. Every drawer, every squirrelled-away box at the top of your wardrobe, each and every pair of shoes, handbag, random sock – everything. Put your worldly fashion possessions on your bed or on the floor and begin to separate into piles of 'like' items, putting blouses, skirts, trousers, etc. together. If you are feeling particularly organised, within these categories also sort into colours – this will be helpful for reasons I will go into later. Apart from accessories, make sure everything will go on a hanger, because the appraisal requires you to hang each item on your rail.

Not all that long ago, I took a trip up to my parents' home, where my mum had sectioned off a tiny corner of the *four* wardrobes in my childhood bedroom for me to hang my clothes (she is the reason I love fashion). All four wardrobes were now filled to the brim with her stuff (fair enough, I haven't lived there for over 20 years!), but she was lost. She has always been a bargain hunter – so had bought lots of pieces because they had been reduced, rather than because they would work with her existing pieces. True story. There wasn't any particular order to them arranged as they were and my mum didn't really have any sense of what it was she owned – it was overwhelming and she wasn't sure how to start putting them together into looks.

So, I began to organise them, separating each similar group into sections: casual tops with casual tops, skirts together, summer trousers in a group with more formal trousers together and so on. It took a few hours, but almost instantly a pattern emerged, with multiple repeat-purchase items evident and also similarities in colour choices. It was obvious the styles she was drawn to, which made it easy to work out what she really needed to keep. With Mum's help, I created charity and resale piles for items she wouldn't wear again, or for those that had started to look, quite literally, worse for wear. Once the rest had been rehung in the wardrobe, still in their categories and further grouped by colour within that, it was clear to see how they could start to be paired.

Hanging clothes up within categories, then further edited by colour groups, you will start to spot your *own* trends. A penchant for a particular colour or print will start to become apparent, or the fact you buy the same shape of skirt or tee shirt. Often you *have* the pieces in your wardrobe; you don't have to buy more – it's just that it's all been thrown/chucked/hidden (you choose the most appropriate verb!) so you can't see the wood for the trees. This is also the case, by the way, if you don't have a huge wardrobe. We become so regimented in our ways that we automatically pair the same pieces together, and it can get a bit boring. Sometimes it just takes fresh eyes to revisit your own wardrobe and consider other combinations that may spice up your life. Well, your outfits at least.

But here's the thing: *try everything on*. It's that classic phrase 'shop your own wardrobe', but you won't be able to do that if you don't know what still works. There is absolutely *no* point in keeping 'good' trousers because you spent a fortune on them five years ago. If you haven't worn them for four of those years, get rid of them. There is *no* good reason to hold on to a lemon-yellow top because it's 'on trend' if it makes you look ill and washed-out. And, as I mentioned earlier, if it no longer fits you, put it to one side – the side that means you won't sneak it back in. You do not need this; it does not bring any kind of fizz to your party.

Appraise your pieces individually and – this is important – take the time to really start listening to your inner voice. We all have one; some are just louder than others. If you fidget, pull things around or just feel uncomfortable, listen to that. That's your inner voice saying, 'There are better things than this for you.' Just put that particular item to the non-party side. When you're ready to put pieces back in your wardrobe, do so in lifestyle sections. Obviously, this is dependent on space, but in a classic wardrobe, this could simply mean different coloured hangers denoting the different areas of clothing along one rail: work, gym, holiday or weekend (I love the coloured non-slip velvet hangers from TK Maxx, around £8 for 25). And stay tuned in to the pieces you are constantly reaching for. One trick is to have all your hangers facing one way, but turning the hanger around when you put back something you've worn. That way the pieces you wear most often will be facing in the opposite direction to the majority.

But the most important piece of advice I can give during this experiment is to stay positive and be kind. It's not *you* who is at fault if something doesn't feel right, it's just the wrong piece for you. You are not 'too big' or 'too small' – you're not 'too' anything – and you don't 'look awful'. You are just you. There is a whole world of choice out there and plenty of pieces that *are* right for you. Put that item to the side because it won't bring you that 'Yes!' happiness we all strive for.

Don't save the best for last

Next, look at your rail and see how many 'saving for best' items of clothing you own. Really, we want to get to a stage where you're not saving *anything* for best. Depending on the kind of look you want to create for yourself – because I really want to encourage the creation of your personal style – try things on in ways you wouldn't usually consider. Think outside the box and start thinking about how *you* want to wear your clothes.

For example, my chosen happy dress length is somewhere between a midi (mid-calf) and maxi (ankle-length), but I have pieces I still love that are around knee-length. In order to get more wear out of those pieces, I wear them over trousers, rather than on their own. Think about your own wardrobe, would you get more wear out of that long silk dress if you threw it on over turned-up jeans? (You could add a belt around the waist if you want to hike it up a little.) Or how about if you paired it with knee-length boots, but wore a silky or thin-rib polo-neck jumper beneath? Would that gorgeous leopard blouse that you only ever wear with black tailored trousers work with that pair of black-and-white spotty palazzo wide legs?

Mixing print and pattern is not to be feared. And doing so can add huge variety to your existing wardrobe. I go into this in a lot more detail in the next chapter. What I really hope you will take from this book (among other things) is self-belief and an ability to rely on your own intuition when it comes to putting together outfits. Fashion doesn't have to be scary.

WHAT TO DO WITH THOSE PIECES THAT NO LONGER WORK FOR YOU

There are going to be plenty of pieces that no longer work for your life and didn't make the cut on the rail. There will probably be quite a few things you bought when you were at home, online shopping, while drinking wine (just me?!), but then didn't get around to returning. We've all been there. There will probably be lots that you've loved but never worn and some that still have the tags on.

There may possibly be some pieces that you bought while hormonal and you're not sure what you were thinking, to be honest. Don't beat yourself up about that! The great thing is that one woman's trash is another's treasure – and there are lots of ways to recycle, donate or make money on your unwanted pieces. Plenty of people use online auction sites like eBay to sell their clothes. But there are lots of others that take the stress out of it, allowing you to be as involved in or removed from the sale as you like. And while most retailers' interest in their clothes stops as soon as you've made the purchase and walked away, more and more brands are beginning to consider the second life of the garments they sell through swapping, recycling and own-brand, pre-loved initiatives – all of which encourage customers to see old clothes in a new way, while doing their bit to save the planet at the same time!

High-street enterprises

OXFAM and **MARKS & SPENCER** are the pioneers of the Shwop. If you bring in your unwanted clothes to Oxfam or the Shwop Drops in M&S stores, you will receive a voucher for money off on clothing, home and beauty products in M&S stores, as long as your donation contains at least one item of M&S-labelled clothing or M&S soft furnishings. You can check online to find out which stores near you offer this service.

H&M has been offering a garment recycling service across all stores since 2013. Their Garment Collecting programme is a global initiative that works to prevent customers' unwanted clothes from going to landfill. They accept unwanted clothes by any brand, in any condition, at any of their stores. You hand in your bag of old clothes at the cash desk and receive a voucher to use towards your next purchase in-store or online. All clothes collected by H&M are either reused, reworn or recycled with 0 per cent going to landfill.

ZARA began installing collection bins in its European stores in 2016 and currently has containers spread across countries including the UK, Spain, Portugal, Ireland, the Netherlands, Denmark and Sweden. The clothes left in the containers are donated to charities such as the Red Cross.

& OTHER STORIES will accept your unwanted clothes, textiles and beauty packaging in their stores in exchange for a voucher.

RIXO LONDON has just launched Rixo Vintage, inviting shoppers to return past-season pieces to their London shop. Customers will then receive money off a new purchase, while their goods will go on to a Rixo-vintage dedicated rail and sell for half price.

LEVI'S, EILEEN FISHER, NIKE and **ADIDAS** all offer a form of return-for-credit or recycling.

CHARITY SHOPS are a great way of moving on those unwanted pieces. As long as items of clothing are clean and in a good condition, charity shops welcome donations. This is also a brilliant and easy way to support your local community.

Donate via digital

VINTED is a great website to sell those high-street buys that still have a tag on. You create a profile, upload images of your item and sell at a price you set. It also offers the chance to swap pieces with other users.

VESTIAIRE COLLECTIVE is for more expensive pieces that will get a higher premium for a savvier shopper. There are two ways to sell: you can either do it yourself, where you submit images of your item, they approve them (and the item), which gives you the green light to upload yourself, or you can use their concierge service, where they come and collect everything from you, take the photos and do all the hard work. This comes with a higher commission, but sellers will receive about 75 per cent of the money their item sells for.

DEPOP is an app that's a cross between eBay and Instagram. It is very popular with teens and 20-somethings who don't want to look like everyone else. It's great for selling high-street pieces. Depop add a 10 per cent commission fee to every sale.

Other initiatives

HURR, BY ROTATION and **MY WARDROBE HQ** are all companies that have created new ways to pass on great-quality pieces that no longer work for you. Their idea is similar to Airbnb, in that users can loan out pieces from their wardrobe to people who pay to borrow them. It's a great way to make money on expensive pieces that may otherwise be sitting in your wardrobe.

FASHION RE:BOOT is a simple, but *brilliant* idea of passing on those old clothes, and means you can make a bit of cash while being sociable to boot. And I say that very modestly, because I co-founded it alongside my friend, former magazine editor Ciara Elliott! Imagine a car-boot sale, but in a hall, hotel or pub, with rails and tables instead of cars – and that's Re:Boot. Events happen all around the UK; check the Instagram page for more information (@fash_reboot).

Alternatively, host your own **CLOTHES SWAPPING PARTY**, where you host, provide the drinks and nibbles, then invite a number of different sized friends around. You should make sure there are defined rules, including the minimum and maximum number of pieces, the condition of the items and when it should take place (end of the season is usually a good time as people are naturally changing over their clothing).

COLOUR ME HAPPY

It's a fashion fact that some colours will suit you more than others. If a colour makes you *look* and *feel* tired, it's the wrong colour for you – no matter how much you love it. Side note: there are lots of companies that offer to 'find' your colours when it comes to clothes, and many do an excellent job I'm sure. However, I have a much simpler strategy – and it doesn't cost a thing. If you hold an item up to your face – in a room with lots of light! – and it suits you, you will be able to see your eyes sparkle and your skin will really glow. If it doesn't, you'll look washed out and a bit tired.

Ditch anything that makes you look or feel tired – and be honest with yourself. And think about colours as tones: don't dismiss an entire colour just because one shade doesn't suit you. For example, while hot pink might drain your colour, blush might make you pop. Or black may really wash you out, but navy or charcoal grey make you feel a million dollars.

While some people are innately attuned to putting together colour combinations, there are plenty who aren't. So, it's all well and good me talking about whether certain colours make you look tired or not, but how do you know what will work if you're shopping online and can't physically hold an item up to your face? There are a couple of natural ways to help figure out the best colours for you, including identifying the darkest and lightest shades within the coloured part of your eye (the iris). They are shades that will always look fantastic on you. Looking at the veins in your wrist can also help – yes, really! If you see blue, then you're more likely to suit cooler colours, while if you see greenish veins, you're suited to warmer shades. There are also practical colour guidelines to help you understand how to wear and combine colours to brilliant effect, rather than clashing and hoping for the best! Once you have a handle on those, you can start to play around with shades that make you happy.

One of the main resources for colour combinations is science – or, more specifically, the traditional colour wheel, which was originally invented by Sir Isaac Newton in the seventeenth century. He passed white light through a prism and watched it fan out into a rainbow, identifying seven constituent colours: red, orange, yellow, green, blue, indigo and violet. A century later, German poet and author Johann Wolfgang von Goethe continued Newton's work with his book *Theory of Colours*, which proposed the idea of a chromatic colour wheel.

Put simply, colours work best when they are in harmony with each other. And there are traditionally five harmonies within the colour wheel that will help you work out those colourful outfit combinations.

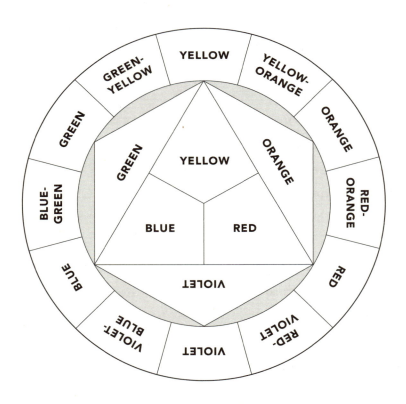

Monochromatic

On my Instagram page, I talk about tonal looks a lot. It's a favourite of mine because the simplicity of the palette makes it a very chic way of wearing one or two very similar shades of colour, for example, cream and camel or navy and sky blue. Technically, it's called a 'monochromatic harmony', meaning a single colour in various gradients. In fashion terms, it always looks fantastic when you incorporate texture, but keep the same colour throughout – a knitted jumper paired with a satin skirt, for example, or a leather jacket mixed with wool trousers.

Complementary

Shades that are complementary to each other are actually, in the world of colour, opposites. If you think about the classic colour wheel, these are the colours that are directly opposite each other, including red and green, violet and yellow, and blue and orange. On paper, they seem a bit full-on, but, in reality, they work really well together and won't seem as 'statement' as you might think. You could try pairing a bright orange blouse with an electric-blue trouser suit and it would look fabulous, for example. Or if that is still a bit too much for your own personal taste, dial down the tones to a more muted coral orange colour and sky blue. Same sides of the colour wheel, just as impactful – dilute to taste.

Neutral

A classic favourite for many, this is when two or more neutral tones, including grey, navy, black, white, cream and brown, are combined. These are arguably the most worn colours, with many of us reaching for a combination of them every day. In turn, they all work together to create a chic, tonal colour palette. And as they are neutral, they work well with brighter shades too, acting as a backdrop to allow other colours to shine.

Analogous

Going back to the idea of the wheel, colours that lie next to each other, or are side by side, are known as analogous colours, such as red, orange and yellow. They're a bit like brother and sister shades, so they work well together because they naturally blend into one another. Traditionally, however, fashion rules dictate that two analogous colours – red and pink – should be kept separate because red is a very warm shade, while pink (in keeping with the family analogy!) is its cooler cousin, and the combo can create an imbalance to the eye. However, red and pink is one of my absolute favourite 'happy' combinations and if you're a fan of a statement look, is definitely one to try. If you'd like to water down the punch slightly, wearing them with denim works to soften and mute the colours, as does teaming with white, which acts as an outfit neutral. You could also wear analogous colours together as accessories if you wanted to dip your toe in and try first.

Triadic

Three shades in the colour wheel that are equal distance apart from each other are known as triadic colours, and they work beautifully together. Lilac, green and orange are good examples to use for this, so you could, say, wear a lilac-coloured jumper with a pale green coat, jeans (acting as your neutral) and orange leather ballet flats, and it would all work in combination. Or if you fancied really going for it, you could try a rust-coloured trouser suit, a purple blouse and dark-green shoes. It's just about playing around and seeing what combinations work for your personal preference.

Working with your skin tone

Apart from looking at the various ways colours harmonise, it is important to consider your own skin tone – which is where the idea of putting colours up to your face comes in. On the traditional colour wheel, where one half (the 'sunset shades') is considered 'warm', the other half is considered 'cool'. Picking colours suited to your own warm or cool skin tone will make the most of your features, make you look bright-eyed and your skin look vital. If you have a yellow skin undertone, choosing warmer shades on both sides of the wheel will be most flattering, including golden yellows, reds, oranges and deep turquoise. For those with a cool or blue skin undertone, navy blue, hot pink and ruby red will flatter your complexion most. As we get older, it's a good idea to rethink the colours that we wear, particularly those worn next to our face, because hair and skin lose pigmentation as we age and bright colours might be a bit overwhelming. But that's not to say you should avoid them – a simple shade shift might be all you need. So, for example, if you loved wearing bright red in your twenties, 40 years later you can still wear a version of that colour, just softened, such as deep pink. It's a really good idea to go through your wardrobe every couple of years and check to see whether the same colour combinations are still working for you. And once you've established the principles, check in with how colours make you feel. You definitely know best.

WHERE TO LOOK FOR STYLE-SPIRATION

For too long style has been seen as the playground and fun zone of the wealthy or those born with supermodel vital stats. It really isn't. Great style comes when you discover the colours and pieces that make you feel fantastic, rather than feeling awkward or out of place in clothes you are wearing to conform or fit in. Practise with the clothes you currently own and see if you can start to develop those skills. Starting off small can help. Quite often I am inspired by one particular colour – which could have been seen on the walls somewhere, or by walking into a store and seeing a colour combination displayed in such a way that it sparks something in the ideas part of my brain.

Seek inspiration everywhere: people on the street, Pinterest, Instagram, magazines – even hotel and restaurant design – might give you an idea for a colour combination you could replicate with your wardrobe. An editor's trick is to create a digital mood board of all the 'looks' that inspire you, saved on Pinterest or to a personal saved folder in Instagram. Pull together the outfits that speak to you and then take note of common themes. From there, try on pieces that emulate those looks and see how you feel when you actually have the clothes on your body. In the beginning of any process there will be a lot of copying, but over time you can refine things and add your own touches, until eventually it becomes uniquely your style. It's overwhelming when you consider the myriad options out there, but sometimes one tiny flower, or cushion, or texture of a rug can spark an idea. It might be looking at a new way of wearing an old favourite and rediscovering it all over again. Just open your mind and your ideas to the possibilities.

FIVE POINTS TO TAKE AWAY

1. Be honest and truthful about what is in your wardrobe. Anything that doesn't fit or you haven't worn in years needs to go.

2. Pay attention to the pieces you reach for time and time again. They're the building blocks of your wardrobe – your outfit superheroes.

3. Taking the time to get your wardrobe organised will really help determine your personal style and make life easier in the long run.

4. You are not at fault if an item of clothing doesn't feel good; it's just the wrong piece for you. There are plenty out there that are right.

5. Don't save occasion wear for occasional wear! Create styling moments where you can re-work or re-wear for more casual days.

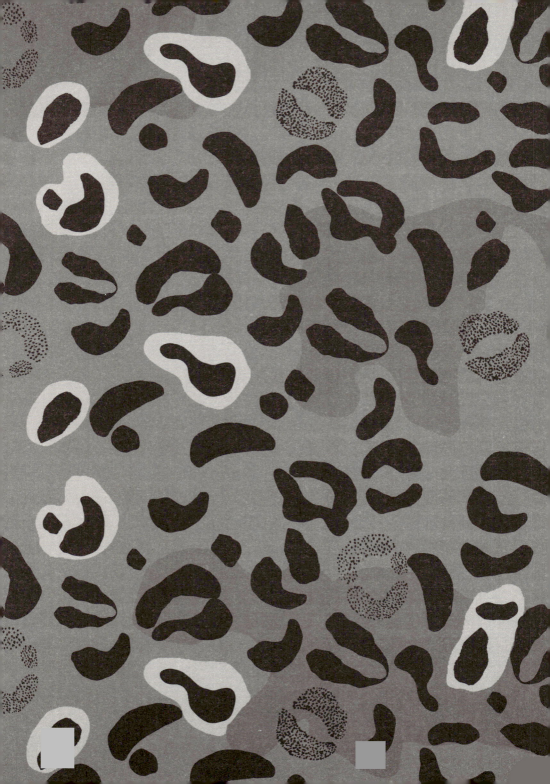

Leopard is a Neutral.
Honestly

CHAPTER FOUR

LEOPARD *IS* A NEUTRAL. HONESTLY

I've never met a leopard print I didn't like.

—Diana Vreeland

It's the title of this book and my go-to statement pattern of choice. It's a print with a history. It's divisive. It's beloved. It's gone from the choice of a *certain type* of woman (please note, the italics represent an eye-roll!) to a pattern now considered a fashion classic. Technically, leopard is a catch-all term for all big cat prints, including cheetah, ocelot or jaguar. Big cat energy, if you will. But since J Crew's former creative director Jenna Lyons announced that 'As far as I'm concerned, leopard is a neutral', the print has been accepted in an entirely new, totally versatile way. And in the context of this book, I am using it as an example of how to more generally incorporate prints into your wardrobe.

Leopard is writ large in my own life. It is a print that has never failed me. I've had animal-print Christmas presents in my stocking since my tweens, my pre-wedding hen party was animal-themed – and I even got married in a pair of leopard Jimmy Choo shoes that my husband had bought me for my thirtieth. Even now, in my forties, I wear the print and it makes me feels cool and sexy and powerful – and seriously, I hope that feeling never leaves me.

Leopard motifs have been used to signify power and confidence for centuries. Let's just take a minute to appreciate its rich and varied history. Egyptian slabs have been found decorated with goddesses wearing leopard or cheetah hide. Seshat, the Egyptian goddess of wisdom, was one such goddess depicted in leopard. In the eighteenth and nineteenth centuries leopard fur and the clothes made from it signified great wealth and status. But it wasn't until the twentieth century, when mass-manufacturing began and synthetic fabrics were readily available, that the print went mainstream.

Now, as then, it's a Marmite pattern: you either love it or you hate it. In popular culture, women wearing the print have been dubbed either femme fatales – and therefore provocative – or tacky. In the UK, this was signified for years by a blousy character called Bet Lynch, in long-running soap opera *Coronation Street*. She was never seen without her leopard coat. An entire generation may still be heard saying, 'Is it a bit Bet Lynch?' when asking for leopard approval. In the US, the character of Peggy Bundy, the morally dubious mother in sitcom *Married . . . with Children*, was similarly find it easy to visualise an outfit. But, after many conversations with colleagues, friends, family members and *plenty* of DM chats with my Instagram followers, I understand that not everyone does and how overwhelming the idea can be. So again, I'm here to tell you that leopard print *is* a neutral, meaning you *can* wear it with everything. It works well with stronger colours, such as jewel shades, neons and even other prints. But equally, the strong black-and-tan pattern stands on its own.

But the thought of it might terrify you – and you can't imagine wearing it on a hair clip, let alone a coat or dress and *God forbid* you consider putting it with other prints! So, let's take it back to basics, to the things you want to touch, feel and wear, then let me help you put new combinations together in a way that feels completely 'you'.

BREAK DOWN THE PRINT

Generally, a traditional leopard print consists of three colours: black, camel and either a lighter cream or darker brown. It's the realistic, yet reconstructed, version of the actual animal skin. But this is fundamentally what you are working with.

Let's say, as an example, that we are holding up a leopard-print blouse. Consider it. You're getting dressed for work – you're standing in front of your wardrobe and trying to work out what to wear. Now, bearing in mind the three colours within the print, there are several classics you could choose here – all good, solid choices, timeless and sophisticated. Let's call these the comfort colours.

Black is probably your default neutral – the one most of us would automatically defer to for a simple, classic look. I would hazard a pretty strong guess that most of us have at least one or two black separates in our wardrobes.

With that in mind, we might think about wearing our blouse with tailored black wide-leg trousers or a plain black A-line skirt, even underneath a black pinafore dress or with black cropped trousers.

Camel and leopard is an equally classic combination. A great camel-coloured coat has to be one of a winter wardrobe's most useful pieces (and there are always plenty of great pre-loved pieces available online – they're a timeless investment). Teaming that leopard blouse with a camel coat works beautifully, or wear it underneath a light-brown or camel trouser suit. Think about layering it beneath a camel cashmere crew-neck jumper, with the collar poking out – adding a hint of playfulness to an otherwise simple outfit.

A dark chocolate brown would also work with our imaginary blouse, even if the print is mainly black and camel. The brown is a lighter tone of the black and a darker tone of the camel, so hits that sweet midway point of matching the tones. Think about wearing with a chocolate brown satin slip skirt or a vintage brown cord blazer. Good, right?

With plains, it all seems easier to style up. Or so you currently think.

Another way of thinking

The idea that leopard is a 'neutral' comes by considering it *exactly* as you would if it were just one of its component colours: the black, the camel or the brown. So, imagine you're still standing there, in front of your wardrobe. What would you choose?

If you want to think about it as black, then go for anything you would wear with black – in whatever texture fabric you'd like, whether that be black leather trousers, a velvet skirt or a cotton knit.

If you want to consider it as part of the brown or camel family, again, you can stick to the classic tone-on-tone varieties of that. Browns and camels look beautiful with sparklier versions of themselves – think about gold, or bronze, or copper; they're part of the family, in the sense that the tones work together, so all the colours harmonise. You could wear the blouse underneath that bronze sequin knit you only pull out for Christmas parties, and then dress the whole look 'down' with denim. Denim has the effect of muting louder, more statement pieces, so they don't feel too 'much' if you want to wear them during the day. But if you do want to make more of a statement, try adding a leather skirt and heels to the mix – a perfect way to make more of the blouse for a night out.

You might have a fabulous gold lurex-threaded vintage coat sitting in your wardrobe passed down from your Great Aunt Beryl – one that's stroked lovingly, but worn rarely. Get it out of that wardrobe! Throw it on with the blouse, a pair of tailored trousers and chunky lace-up brogues. Turn that vintage heirloom into something that works with your blouse for a cool day look that's bound to prompt a few 'Where did you get that from?' questions.

But you can also push the envelope a little. Step away from the comfort of the family. Look at pairing the blouse with lilac and red, blush pink or bright orange. Leopard works with all of those shades, because the three main colours within the print work with all of those shades. How about a lilac single-breasted coat worn over the blouse, teamed with your favourite pair of black trousers? Or an orange knit worn over the top of it, then teamed with a brown leather midi skirt and knee-high boots.

It's really not as scary as you might think. Honestly. And once you have considered the options of stepping away from the comfort colours, you might be ready for mixing with other prints – and for a myriad other outfit possibilities.

MIXING IT WITH OTHER PRINTS

I think it was Carrie Bradshaw who started it all for me. Print clashing, I mean. The wardrobe of the *Sex and the City* character, played by Sarah Jessica Parker, has been woven into fashion folklore. The character (or author Candace Bushnell) even penned one of the most oft-recited fashion quotes of all time: 'I like my money right where I can see it – hanging in my closet.'

Take the opening credits of the late-nineties/early-noughties HBO TV classic as an example. Carrie struts down a Manhattan sidewalk wearing a tight, blush-pink bodysuit, tulle skirt and Manolo Blahnik sandals and is sprayed by a bus driving through a puddle, before seeing her image on the side of it. That whole visual sums up Carrie's sense of style to me: whimsical, fearless, feminine, cool, emotional and totally unapologetic.

As a fashion editor, I would often write style features around big TV shows such as this one, and because it was such a hit I flew to New York to interview the series stylist – and visionary behind Carrie's wardrobe – Patricia Field. The 78-year-old style veteran brought her own particular irreverent, downtown New York style to the show, with its mix of high-end and vintage, designer and thrift pieces – all the while showing millions of women how to confidently express themselves through their wardrobe.

I sat down with her at her eponymous boutique on 8th Street, a store now closed, but then filled to the brim with clubbing, punk, fetish and vintage pieces, with feather boas, huge gold hoop earrings and nameplate necklaces – just like the one Carrie wore. While Field pioneered the high-end lending between TV shows and designers such as Stella McCartney, Christian Lacroix and Christian Dior (previously they had to buy specific pieces on a budget), her love of vintage shone through. She told me her team specifically targeted the vintage stores in Miami for Carrie's wardrobe, where there was a 'ton' of great stuff.

She said: 'I personally believed the audience loved a high-low look – a mix of designer and vintage – because that was something new and interesting on TV and also attainable. It was more about style than fashion design – a real person's wardrobe, but with imagination.' I *was* that audience and I *did* love that mix. It was a light-bulb moment – why couldn't I wear *that* floral blouse with *that* animal-print skirt? Who said I shouldn't?

It made me reconsider that high street isn't the only option. That vintage and second-hand pieces can add huge amounts of personality – and individuality – to your look. That a designer bag, or a pair of shoes or a sentimental hand-me-down does the same. That the sum of all these fashion parts is what is *fun* about style. That it doesn't have to be new; sometimes it just has to be new to *you*. And often, all it takes is one person to inspire you – in my case, two: Carrie *and* Patricia.

LEOPARD *AND* STRIPES?

One thing Patricia showed was that, really, there aren't any rules when it comes to style. The character of Carrie Bradshaw demonstrated that every day can be a 'fashion moment' if you have confidence. Field has even said: 'costume design isn't about selling clothes, it's about telling a story'. And if you apply those principles to your own life, by selecting outfits that make you happy with your own story, you can be whoever you want to be. It doesn't always have to be by wearing the Insta-hit of the moment or the designer 'must-have'.

I've sat across from women at fashion shows who are dressed head to toe in one designer. Now common sense would suggest that's because they've been dressed *to attend* the show, but it could also be that they're the women buying the designer's creations season after season, showing that they're a certain type of woman with a certain type of budget. It's interesting because I have never really understood that type of expensive uniform dressing. Wearing conspicuous logos and labels, for me, speaks of wanting to belong, to be seen and show the world that you 'know'. But for them, it's perhaps a type of armour – a way of feeling powerful and in control.

Personally, I believe an outfit says more about a person when they mix everything up, perhaps a bit of designer (budget willing) here, a splash of vintage there. There is cachet these days in being seen not to have spent very much on an outfit, but still looking amazing. It could be a vintage petticoat slip dress worn over a striped tee with a denim jacket thrown over your shoulders and your favourite sandals, or a charity-shop retro tee worn with a satin maxi skirt. It could be a simple black shift dress worn with chunky trainers. It's about creating your own sartorial joy. What is important is your reaction to the piece and how it makes you feel when you put it on.

I couldn't go through this chapter without mentioning again one of my style favourites, a true fashion creative and someone whose outfits, for me, always spark sartorial joy and inspiration: Jenna Lyons. Jenna is a female creative tour de force and someone who has completely nailed the everyday fashion moment brief, with an instinctive and inspiring approach to personal style. If you aren't aware of her work, Google her. Honestly, there are Internet pages dedicated to her geek-chic quirkiness and penchant for mixing camo with stripes and sequins, feminine tulle maxi skirts with slouchy, cashmere V-necks, or layered khaki army jackets beneath shoulder-draping leopard coats. She is fearless in the juxtaposition of contrasting pieces. She makes the art of getting dressed fun.

Jenna clashes up the prints with confidence, but that's

because she has her own style locked down. It takes time to develop it, so go at your own pace and see where it takes you. How would you feel about trying our imaginary leopard-print blouse with a pair of black and brown houndstooth trousers? Yes, another pattern – but there is consistency with the same colours in both. This is what it all comes down to for me: start off by mixing prints with similar tones and colours. They can be completely and utterly distinctive in design or texture, but it won't jar because the eye automatically connects the matching colours, rather than being confused by the different patterns. Using that principle, you can start to look at other separates and create new outfits. Here are some outfit suggestions for our blouse:

- A black-and-beige spotty skirt
- A brown striped skirt
- Under a black-and-brown floral strappy dress
- Herringbone trousers, either brown or black or both
- Gold snake-printed metallic skirt (because, as we discussed earlier, the gold is in the family)
- Worn *over* a beige-and-black striped long-sleeved tee with black jeans
- With a long, maroon-coloured tulle skirt and a black striped clutch bag (here the stripe is the additional pattern)

Don't let pattern intimidate you – just do as much or as little as you like. If it makes you happy, try it. What have you got to lose?

FIVE POINTS TO TAKE AWAY

1. Leopard *is* a neutral, meaning you can wear it with everything.
2. Vintage and second-hand pieces can add huge amounts of personality and individuality to your look.
3. When wearing prints, wear denim if you want to tone things down a little.
4. Your outfits should tell your own story.
5. Create your own sartorial joy. What is important is your reaction to a piece of clothing and how it makes you feel when you put it on.

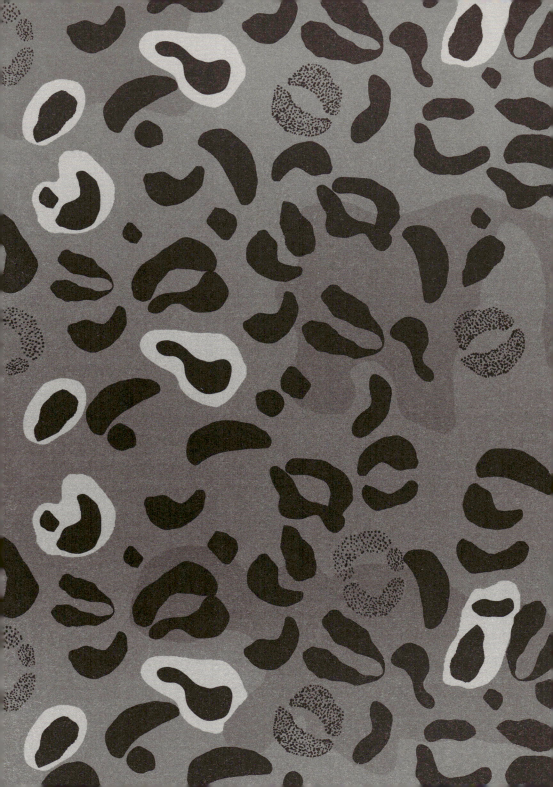

Finding Your Comfort Zone

CHAPTER FIVE

FINDING YOUR COMFORT ZONE

Anyone can get dressed up and glamorous, but it is how people dress in their days off that are the most intriguing.
—Alexander Wang

I've never been one of the cool girls. I hoped I would be, but I've always been too keen to make friends to be able to rock that insouciant stand-offish thing that cool girls have! I tried, I really tried. I tried the fashion trends, but most didn't suit me. I wore flares that fitted tightly around my thighs before zooming out from the knee; I chose velvet jeans worn with scoop-neck tees and waistcoats; and I preferred baggy cardigans and DM boots to bodycon frocks! I had *all* the haircuts – a low point being 'The Rachel' on my naturally thick, curly hair in the days before I could handle a hairdryer. I wore Rimmel's frosted Heather Shimmer lipstick, because everyone else did, even though that was a *really* bad idea against my sallow skin.

It was easier to accept my lack of coolness fairly early on, because, to be frank, it made things a lot easier, forcing me into carving out my own sartorial path. While I admire things (all the time!) on other people, I know they wouldn't be right for me – because I now know that, after years of trying, the clothes they look amazing in won't make *me* feel amazing.

My coolness begins and ends with this one sentence: I love the idea of getting dressed up and going out, but always secretly plan when I can leave, go home and put my pyjamas on. And actually, I don't care. I am very comfortable with wanting to *be* comfortable. I am happy to say, 'No thank you' if I don't want to do something. I am comfortable enough to know that putting myself through the hoopla doesn't make me want to high-five myself for being cool, it just makes me feel anxious and out of sorts. Not listening to my internal voice saying, 'Don't do it' or 'Don't wear it' makes me feel rubbish about my decision-making skills. After all, why do we tell our children to trust their gut if we ignore our own?

And yet, there is something inherently cool about comfort. And I don't just mean in a sweatpant and slouchy knit kind of a way – although, wait, we'll get there. Being comfortable with who you are is a big deal. It's where we are all aiming to get to. To me, being comfortable means not comparing yourself to others and being at ease with whatever choices you make in life. It means accepting how you look, how much you weigh, accepting that, yes, your thighs rub together a little, or that they don't. It's about being OK with the grey hairs that sprout like a fuzzy little halo around your crown. It's remembering to keep tweezers handy for when the chin hairs erupt from out of nowhere. It's about having self-esteem and those one or two *great* friends you can call at any time of the day or night. It's about being content with where you are in your life. But at the core of it all is the very strong sense that you are fine just as you are. When you're truly comfortable with yourself, you don't feel the need to compare – and you don't feel you have to do things to try to impress others. And honestly, this is *so* important. Trying to please everyone is exhausting and pointless. In fact, it'll hold you back from your full potential. Accept that not everyone will like you, so don't even try – and move on with what it is *you* want to do.

It's hard, though, because we are all constantly bombarded with images and suggestions from 'perfect lives' on our smartphones and social media accounts, all showing us what we 'should' be doing and how we 'need' to spend our time and what we 'have' to wear. It wasn't like that when I was a teenager, when we just had magazines and the TV! It can make us feel as though our own life isn't quite hitting the bar. I understand, because I feel it too. On Instagram, someone else's day might look much better than mine – even when up until that point I have been having a perfectly lovely time.

Obsessing over glamorous lives online or photographs of

clothes worn by influencers and on magazine pages definitely drives a very strong sense of comparison culture. It creates the idea of 'I need that now in order to be happy' or to 'be like them'. It stops us fully appreciating the things we do have. We completely lose sight of what's important because, to our slightly warped mindset, happiness is what *other* people have. It's absolutely crucial to take time to set boundaries and focus on ourselves. It would be so helpful to stop ourselves thinking that our lives have to be filled at all times with excitement and events. But it's hard when social media doesn't switch off, because, often, neither do we. But really, some of the happiest moments could be considered *just that* during the most mundane of activities. Probably without your phone. Definitely wearing sweatpants.

Previously, style rules have talked about 'comfort' in fashion being practical or, worse, boring. German designer Karl Lagerfeld – famous for his barbed comments – once said that sweatpants 'were a sign of defeat'. But comfort in fashion is intrinsically linked to that sense of self. Think about the times when you are really comfortable with what you're wearing. Is it wearing jeans and a slouchy tee, or a fitted dress with smart heels? Is it when you're curled up on the sofa watching TV in your cosy trousers and those really old cashmere socks? Or wearing a dress that doesn't pull around your belly to a really lovely lunch out with friends? Or is it when you're nailing a meeting at work wearing your lucky pants and a fitted trouser suit?

A sense of comfort in fashion really does come from feeling appropriate for the occasion, as well as the physical comfort you gain from wearing clothes that fit well. I am not suggesting we all live in elasticated waist trackpants and sweatshirts, but neither do I agree with Lagerfeld's 'sign of defeat' comment. I firmly believe that comfort is just as integral as aesthetics when it comes to developing personal style. It allows you to take ownership of what it is you *want* to wear, without the constraints of what you *think* you should be wearing, or what you *think* other people want to see you in.

THE RISE OF 'ATHLEISURE'

Interestingly, the loungewear and athleisure industry is a constantly growing category of clothing. It hasn't shared any of the patterns of growth experienced by other parts of the fashion industry, whereby a market booms, reaches saturation point and then starts to slow down. Instead, athleisure and the entire 'wellness' industry is expanding, so much so that industry predictions expect it to have a value of $257 billion by 2026. From basic black leggings sold even five years ago, it's now selling phenomenally expensive patterned ones aimed predominantly at women, built out of the habits of stay-at-home mums, students and fitness professionals, who all wear exercise clothing outside of an exercise setting, carving out a stylish (previously performance) space between function and comfort.

'Wellness' is a very broad term and can be considered as more about your state of mind than the fact you might practise yoga and make your own smoothie each morning. Wearing products such as performance leggings or yoga pants gives that person the 'association' of taking part in a healthy activity, whether they are or not. It's definitely a look that expresses an aspiration for health. I don't know about you, but on my own school run in the morning, a huge majority of the mums dropping off do so wearing gym gear. It's easy and it's comfortable. Key word. Over the last few years alone, high-street brands have unveiled new specialist athleisure ranges – with gym-appropriate iterations of their trademark style (leopard print and camouflage, anyone?). Marks & Spencer has its 'Goodmove' range, which features knit trainers that would look just as good with jeans as with leopard leggings, and a slim-fit hoody I'd pair with a skirt and blazer, not just my gym kit. ARKET's running collection features the most stylish fleece I have ever seen – and one I'd be very happy to wear outside of the gym. With double-duty pieces making their way into mainstream collections like these, there's a blurred line between performance wear and casual wear and you can start to see why this industry is booming. Equally, most major brands are now creating loungewear collections, aimed at 'improving the lives' of women who do spend a lot of time in the home. Actually, I think it's less about improvement and more about creating a demand for something you previously didn't know you needed. Who wants to wear their partner's jogging pants and a tee shirt on a Sunday night, when they can have their own cashmere loungewear?!

But these examples serve to prove that, once again, women are sold to. Even basic human functions, such as exercising or, conversely, flopping on the sofa at home, have become part of a competitive sales arena. You 'need' expensive brands – your Lululemon leggings, LAPP tracksuit, your Vaara sports bra. You 'have to' have a soothing grey pair of N.Peal cashmere lounge pants and a hoody to match. You 'need' Olivia von Halle designer pyjamas or Desmond & Dempsey shorties, monogrammed with your initials. You *need* them, otherwise you're doing exercise and lounging all wrong!

Fashion really isn't about how much something costs, or whether someone else thinks you need it. It's really not about wearing the 'must-have' dress. Of course, you can buy that dress, or those sports leggings or that cashmere – as long as your finances allow and they make you feel good – but you never want to get to a stage where you're trying to keep up with someone else. We all have different budgets and place importance on different things within our own lives. It's why now, on social media, I try to steer clear of using the buzzwords of my previous print-fashion-editor existence – words including 'affordable', 'must-have', 'budget' or 'value'. I have learned that while some shoppers would *never* buy a piece of knitwear costing over £100, for example, another group of people would prefer to do that because they are looking at it from a completely different perspective – they may not buy so many pieces and want clothes that last; they may want to invest in a company that has a more sustainable business model; or they may have more disposable income and choose to spend it on their clothing. There are lots of reasons for people's shopping habits – and that's a decision for them to make. In short, you do you!

It's all about the importance of your own personal priority list. It's simply not my business to decide what is or isn't affordable to someone reading my page. I believe what you should do, as an editor with an audience, is provide examples of pieces you personally have a response to, discuss the reasons for that response and allow the people who enjoy what you 'edit' to make up their own mind, whether that involves swiping up and buying the same item, or shopping around and finding a similar piece that works for their own budget or shopping beliefs.

The brilliant thing about social media is that we have the choice to follow and connect with like-minded people, so the likelihood is that you will appreciate the taste levels of those you follow. You will look to people with a similar body shape, or who wear brands you personally love, and allow their taste to edit the high street for you. I do think it's important to keep curating the people whom you follow – checking in with yourself to make sure they don't make you feel in any way sold to, or lacking in your own skin or wardrobe.

That sense of being happy in the skin you're in has a huge impact on your style. If you feel comfortable in what you are wearing, it will show in your posture and your appearance. Consider the pieces you own that instantly make you feel cosy and warm, or chic and sexy – as soon as you put them on. That's a great place from which to start building the kind of look you want to present yourself in. They give you a great idea about the shapes, fits and even details of the kind of material or textures you are drawn to. I have learned over the years that I really don't like thick, woollen polo necks, for example. I don't mind thin ones for layering, but I feel constricted and overheat instantly in thick knits – or I imagine that I am getting a rash all over my chin from the wool. Speaking of wool, I don't like it pure and unadulterated. I get a bit itchy and scratchy and want to take it off immediately. Mixed with other fabrics it's fine, but not on its own. However, I love cashmere crew necks – they're my classic comfort go-to – and I repeat-buy and wear until they fall apart. Or at least, until the moths get them! (Top tip: try buying men's cashmere crew-neck jumpers for a more modern slouch. You tend to find more 'classic' colours within the men's departments, which work perfectly for tonal outfits and also to ground louder, more print-heavy looks.)

Look for cashmere out of season (on websites such as THE OUTNET, for example). Some of the best prices will be at the wrong time of year and therefore slightly cheaper. Also, don't forget to look at second-hand options for cashmere jumpers and cardigans. Choose brands that would have previously retailed at a high price point because then you'll be able to appreciate the quality. Don't buy anything that's stained or beyond repair (a few little stitches aren't enough to put me off, but anything that requires a lot more work may not be worth it), and for pilling on a vintage piece, it's easy to remove using a blunt razor gently across a taut jumper, or invest in a cashmere comb or fabric shaver – they can really save your knits!

Developing a style that makes you happy is as important as how good you feel wearing it. Comfort is indeed king. Or queen. And it can be as simple as finding a specific shape of clothing or, as mentioned above, a specific piece that makes you feel comfortable and like 'you'. I am curvier on my bottom half, so for years I followed all the 'rules' for dressing as such. I bought fitted knits and wider skirts, to 'make the most of my smaller waist' – until I realised that, for me, a slouchier knit felt cooler and more comfortable. At five foot five, knee-length skirts made me feel frumpy – I simply felt more relaxed and preferred myself in styles that hit the calf or were longer.

And here's the big one: I stopped wearing jeans, because they never felt right on me. I had tried every trend, from vintage 501s, to skinny to 'mom' and always felt awkward and self-conscious with how I looked in them. It was undoubtedly due to my own body insecurities – and a vocal 'friend' telling me my bum looked 'too big' in them. But I battled on, because everyone wears jeans, right?! Wrong. I simply stopped forcing everyone else's casual style on myself and found other trousers to bridge the gap. I found carrot-shaped denim styles (wider around the thighs, more tapered towards the ankle), wide-leg jersey pairs and boyfriend-shape khaki chinos (looser around the waist and thigh, slimmer down the leg).

Note here: you really don't have to do what everyone tells you. In the classic 'mum' phrase of old, if everyone else put their hand in the fire, would you do it too? Jeans just might not be the most 'you' casual piece you could wear – and *that's OK*. There will be, as I've mentioned above, other trouser shapes that are. Sometimes it's just a case of finding the right shape and fit for you – there will always be one that suits; it may just be worth spending some time in-store trying things on. Or, you could do what a former work colleague does and only ever stick to dresses and skirts, even at weekends. It's your choice. For me, narrowing down the shapes that made me feel good meant I could instantly dismiss pieces when I went shopping – which cut down on the aimless meandering around shop floors. More on this later.

In the past, Italian fashion design powerhouse Donatella Versace has said: 'to be comfortable, that can't be in the vocabulary of fashion. If you want to be comfortable, stay home in your pyjamas.' If that's the case then I'm happy to embrace the fashion JOMO (Joy Of Missing Out) and stick to my personal style. As Coco Chanel said: 'fashion has two purposes, comfort and love. Beauty comes when fashion succeeds.' I couldn't agree more with this statement. Comfort and love. Could there be two more, well, comforting and loving words? And one of the most notable fashion designers in history – whose work is still inspiring a generation – suggests that in order to be 'fashionable', our outfits need to tick both of those boxes. Not a feeling of discomfort, or grudging acceptance, or a sense of 'everyone else is, so I should'. Not how I felt in my jeans!

GETTING DOWN TO THE BASICS

Anyway, Donatella may be missing a trick because sleepwear, the most comfortable clothing around, is big business – in and out of the bedroom. Ukrainian brand Sleeper has quietly become a cult hit, specialising in coordinating sets with feather trims. And while they were originally created for fancy sleepwear, celebrities and digital content creators have quickly repurposed them for party-wear – just adding heels, red lipstick and statement earrings. Department store Liberty London even redesigned their entire sleepwear collection after spotting a huge hike in their year-on-year growth. And YOLKE – another sleepwear brand for whom printed silky slips and PJ sets are just too lovely to hide under the duvet – says the double-duty wearing of posh pyjamas gives a nod to the fact that more people are trying to buy pieces that will last and they will wear more often. Also, Kate Moss wore their matchy-matchy leopard silk shirt and trouser combination out recently, which sealed this particularly cosy deal.

So yes, forget the FOMO (Fear Of Missing Out) – we have definitely turned into a generation of JOMO-lovers. And when streaming TV channels in the comfort of our very own homes has turned many of us into antisocial beings (again, just me?!), there's little wonder so many of us are big into the comfort factor of loungewear. Be comfy; look cute while you're doing it.

Underwear is a *big* part of getting the comfort right. I'm probably not alone in getting home and immediately whipping off my bra. In fact, I know I'm not. Underwear brand Sloggi conducted a survey in which 45 per cent of British women said they were so uncomfortable in their bras by the end of the day, taking them off was the first thing they did when they got home. I also can't be the only woman who has a bra 'wardrobe' – a black lace one for nights out, smooth tee shirt bras in skin tone for everyday wear and a couple of brighter coloured bras in case I want to show a little of the strap under a top or dress.

What I don't have are multiple drawers of matching lingerie. I never have done. In fact, my underwear is boringly useful – and yes, comfortable. And, actually, embarrassingly old. Nora Ephron once wrote that she felt 'bad about her neck'. Well, I feel bad about my pants. More so for my husband! *Nothing* matches, unless I happen to be wearing a skin-tone bra and a pair of pants in a similar shade. I take myself off to be measured by a professional every couple of years and invest in a few new bras, but generally I'm not a huge purchaser of lingerie. I actually wish I was. Perhaps when I grow up I will be. I have a friend who only ever wears gorgeous, expensive and *matching* sets of lingerie because that's what her mother taught her to do. 'What if you get run over and they have to cut you out of your clothes?' she asked me. 'Wouldn't you be mortified that you're wearing pants with holes in?' In that situation, I'm not sure my underwear would be my first consideration, to be honest, but I take her point.

Perhaps I am giving too much credence to that oft-cited cliché of 'nice' undies being that itchy red lace underwear set, usually given (by a partner) at Christmas or on Valentine's Day, in a not-so-subtle way of suggesting a couple's love life needs spicing up. Today women are far less susceptible to that kind of marketing (if they ever were). The idea of what is 'sexy' has completely changed. You don't need to get all trussed up (unless you want to) because the choice of so-called sexy lingerie has become so much more than just lace and push-ups. Innovation in stretchy elastics, super-soft cups and brushed fabrics has elevated comfort to a whole other level in the lingerie arena, so we just don't 'need' to make do with the traditional parameters of pretty underwear – the choice is out there, we can make our own rules up. It's all part of creating that wardrobe of lingerie.

Just as you might open your wardrobe and ask yourself

'who you want to be' that day, you may also open up your underwear drawer and decide whether your day requires a thong or a pair of non-VPL waist-height pants. Your day, your choice. Most women these days don't want to have to worry about – or be conscious of – underwear lines, so seam-free, smoothing and *comfortable* underwear in neutral skin tones are bestsellers. Knickers that won't disappear up your bum at an inopportune moment, bras that won't dig or cause discomfort while you're trying to give a presentation, basically, underwear that doesn't feel as though you're wearing underwear – this is the *new* definition of sexy.

Brands such as Commando, The KiT, Bodas, Nubian Skin, Baserange and Kim Kardashian West's SKIMS collection all offer minimalist, everyday basics, fuss-free pieces designed to balance the need for comfort, stretch and support. Their bamboo, modal, microfibre-blend, seam-free, skin-toned pieces might not add a flowery flourish to your foundation garments, but I, for one, am no longer looking for that. I'm happy with minimalist and basic and stretchy. Those pieces feel more modern to me and, yes, sexy. There's power in taking back the comfort of your lingerie – rather than wearing the kind of feminine underwear we've been told we need to wear in order to make ourselves more appealing.

But you know what? I don't want to sound holier than thou when it comes to the perceptions of sexiness and lingerie. Because that's not my intention. As with everything I am trying to say in this book, the decision-making process of what you want to wear – and the power that creates – is yours and yours alone. And if, like my friend, you prefer a patterned, pretty or sexy matching set, because they make you feel sexy and strong and in control (and, of course, in case you ever get run over – although, I'm keeping everything crossed that that *never* happens), check out brands like Lonely, Hanky Panky, Dora Larsen, Fleur of England, Les Girls Les Boys and Stripe & Stare. All of them are designed with a modern woman in mind – and are definitely worth considering alongside your more usual high-street offerings.

THE COMFORTABLE LITTLE DETAILS THAT WILL MAKE A BIG DIFFERENCE TO YOUR OUTFIT

Tailoring

Making things fit you will open up a whole new world, whether it's a vintage find on an auction website or a high-street sale bargain that could do with being taken up a little. Find someone to tweak (through local recommendation, a Facebook search or by asking in a local haberdashery) or learn to do it yourself, either at a local dressmaking class or via the wonders of a YouTube tutorial. A little altering can make the world of difference, as though you've had it made to measure.

A very petite friend of mine never discounts anything maxi-length on her shopping travels, even though she knows she will have to take at least six inches off the bottom. She buys and immediately takes it to her local seamstress to have it altered. Another male friend – who is an absolute demon for tracking down amazing pieces on eBay – has found himself a brilliant tailor who tweaks and nips the slightly-too-big Tom Ford jackets he's found or takes in the waistband on never-been-worn Aquascutum trousers to make sure they fit perfectly. Little details like this can make a *big* difference. You can be wearing the simplest pieces in the world, but adding a tweak, or a couple of well-considered accessories, elevates them from basic to you.

Lingerie and shapewear

Do yourself a huge favour – go and get yourself professionally fitted for a bra. You might think you know your size, but the reality is, you were last told you were a 34B in 1995 and things *may* have shifted somewhat since then. In my experience, it's best to try somewhere that sells a variety of different brands, so you are able to then try on, well, a variety of different bras. Take the time to really consider the comfort of each – if something is pulling or scratching during the try-on stage, it's never going to get any better (life lesson there). Alongside a decent sports bra, here is the holy trinity of bras you should have in your wardrobe:

1.   A skin-toned tee shirt bra that has thick enough material across the front so as not to let any cold nipples join the party.
2.   A black bra, possibly with a little bit of lace at the top, to wear under dark tops and dresses, but also to wear as your 'going out' bra.
3.   A coloured bra, whether in a muted jewel tone or a neon bright – just something that warrants a little flash should the mood take you and you fancy wearing something that'll show it off a bit.

With shapewear I am conflicted. I love the brands mentioned above offering minimal, cool and practical support, that also look at 'shapewear solutions'. Previously these have been the restrictive, tight-fitting, don't-even-think-about-going-to-the-toilet styles that are 'guaranteed to make you look a dress size smaller'. They've turned entrepreneurs with a simple idea into multimillionaires – and 9 million pairs of SPANX footless body-shaping tights have been sold since the brand's launch in 2000. Now, I do understand that sometimes the choice of wanting to wear a supportive piece of lingerie comes from a desire to boost your self-confidence. You may be wearing a tighter dress than usual and want a more supportive pair of pants, a slip or even tights, so you feel more put-together. But the thing I want to shout really loudly here is: 'You do *not* need to look a dress size smaller!' However, there is more to shapewear than looking 'slimmer'. Clever lingerie beneath your outfit can do all sorts of things – from making see-through fabrics a little more modest to stopping jersey dresses from pulling or sagging, and they can help you work out your options for a dress that can't be worn with a normal pair of knickers. A few winning pieces from different underwear specialists can not only make you feel more pulled-together (literally), but they cover a lot of bases.

HEIST TIGHTS AND BODYSUITS: Heist came on to the fashion scene with their game-changing range of tights, that, in their words, 'liberated women from disappointing underwear'. They only use durable yarns and do without seams and gussets, making digging and sagging a thing of the past. They have also launched the Outer Body, a bodysuit that smooths and supports in a small range of colours you wouldn't mind showing off.

CAPEZIO FISHNET DANCE TIGHTS: If they're all right for Beyoncé, they're all right with me! These super-thick fishnets are brilliant because they don't look thick, yet give the leg a really defined look. They're also long-lasting because they're designed for dancers, so are ladder-resistant.

WACOAL LONG LEG SHAPER: This is actually called 'curve control long leg shaper', but I'm OK with controlling my curves, thanks. I do, however, occasionally need something that'll work if I want a smooth look without VPL and I find this pair the most comfortable.

MAIDENFORM WAIST NIPPER: Previously worn to create an hourglass shape, these can disguise a premenstrual bloat or, when worn beneath satin, silky or sequin dresses, they ensure that they sit well and don't ride up.

FASHION FORMS VOLUPTUOUS SILICONE LIFT BRA: This stick-on wonder is a full-busted, adhesive, backless bra, perfect if you want to go backless but have large breasts that need support. It has transparent and convertible straps that can be turned into a halterneck. Reusable if you handwash with soap and water, leave to air-dry and keep in its original packaging.

DOMINIQUE'S 'NOEMI' BUSTIER: This longline bustier is backless, yet offers support if you want to wear a backless dress or top. It's also available in black and ivory, but does only go up to an E cup. Wear with high-waist pants so it gives a streamlined look under your clothes.

MARKS & SPENCER CULOTTES WITH COOL COMFORT TECHNOLOGY: Like a slip, to wear under a flimsy dress, but with the non-chafing benefit of being culottes. I think these culottes are one of the most useful pieces in my underwear drawer – particularly if you suffer a bit with your thighs rubbing together when wearing skirts or frocks.

Now back to some other style suggestions . . .

Ignore the size

It's easy to get wrapped up in the numbers game, but honestly, it *really* doesn't matter to anyone but you. The world still turns regardless of what size you wear. Going up a size will often make a piece feel more comfortable because you're not constantly pulling or tugging at certain areas. Also, plenty of fashion editors I know do this anyway, because clothes that are slightly looser are often more flattering. Just because you can zip or button up something, doesn't mean it will be comfortable. Learn to trust your instincts about fit – and don't stress about the number on the label. Honestly, no one cares.

Develop something signature

I have a friend who says that if she wakes up and doesn't feel good about herself, she needs a bit of a self-confidence boost – and all it takes for her to get her mojo back is to put on her gold hoop earrings and a spritz of 'Pomelo' by Jo Loves. She says the hoops are like some kind of magic talisman that'll give her an instant lift and the scent just makes her feel better. For me, it's a red lipstick. I have several brands that I turn to, depending on the time of year (if you're interested, MAC's 'Lady Danger' in the summer and Louboutin Beauty's 'Altressa Velvet Matte' during the winter!). Or, eyebrows. If my eyebrows have been threaded, I can cope with the world. It's a little bit of self-care that just makes me feel more in control.

There are very quick style fixes that will help create a more unique look, so don't discount pieces when you're out shopping immediately because there's always a way of making it work! It could be a colour you always like to incorporate in some way, or a style of shirt that makes you feel pulled-together. It might be a pair of glasses, or a way of defining your waist. Often, it's a more singular thing that becomes your signature – a hair colour, or style (think Anna Wintour), or even a piece of jewellery. Sticking with a bold shade of lipstick is a basic signature, but also one that's a no-brainer – even with the simplest of outfits, or in a strange environment, it will give you comfort and make you feel like yourself.

Listen to your own internal voice, no one else's

How many times have you put something on and felt great, only to have someone else's comment about it make you feel instantly awkward? Learning to only listen to your internal voice is one of the best tips I can give you in order to be truly comfortable. Any garment will look amazing if you're really happy and comfortable wearing it – whether it's a pair of tracksuit bottoms or an evening gown. My happiness in an outfit is often when I know I have nailed it for a particular occasion – be it a meeting, an event, or even the school run. If you're comfortable and feel appropriate, you will feel it. So, don't let anyone dictate to you what you should or shouldn't wear. Let your style be determined by who you are and not who others say you should be.

It's a massive cliché, but just do you. Have fun dressing for yourself – and you might be surprised at the reaction you receive when you just own it!

FIVE POINTS TO TAKE AWAY

1. Comfort is about being at ease with your own choices; in life and clothing – not comparing yourself to others.

2. Anything you put on will look amazing if you feel happy and comfortable wearing it.

3. On social media, constantly curate the people you follow, regularly check in with yourself to make sure they don't make you feel in any way lacking in your own skin.

4. The simplest things can make the biggest difference to how you feel – whether it's a spritz of your favourite perfume or a properly fitting bra.

5. No one else scrutinises you as much as you scrutinise yourself. Don't hold yourself back by dressing for people who don't care enough to notice.

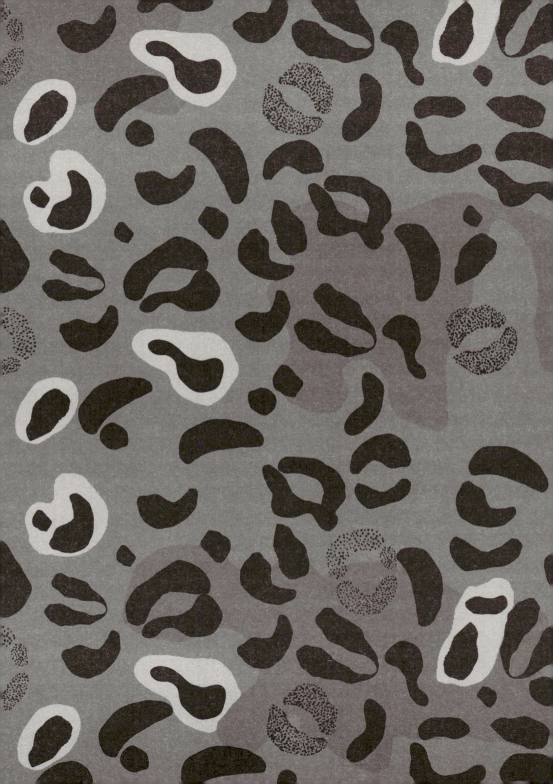

How to "Scan" the Shops like a Fashion Editor

CHAPTER SIX

HOW TO 'SCAN' THE SHOPS LIKE A FASHION EDITOR

What you wear is how you present yourself to the world, especially today, when human contacts are so quick. Fashion is instant language.

—Miuccia Prada

We have considered who we want to show ourselves to be with our personal style, got to grip with prints and looked at the importance of comfort in what you wear. Now let me show you how you to take those principles and apply them when you're out shopping, or sitting at home online with your fingers itching to press 'buy now'.

I really believe there is an art to shopping. And it isn't one that means methodically working your way around stores and their merchandised rails. It is about trusting your instincts on pieces, rather than following the crowd. It's not about sticking to one brand or one store, but listening to your gut and seeking out pieces that give you an immediate feeling. It doesn't matter if it's new, old or slightly battered around the edges – what matters is that you had a response to it. When it comes to shopping for new-season styles, try to buy or find pieces that will seamlessly work with what you already have in your wardrobe, so they don't stand out too much. With trends – just like with statement pieces – it's about you wearing *them*, rather than *them* wearing you.

Creating your style is a labour of love. Anyone can steal a look straight off the catwalk. But, it takes an eye to interpret the catwalks and formulate an original look – perhaps mixing a little high-street piece you've had for years with that designer buy, or adding a vintage twist to an existing outfit. Coming at clothing with an open mind and a willingness to experiment makes a difference to the way you will shop for things, too. I'd never turn my nose up at a cheap find on a random market stall, in the same way I wouldn't automatically discount something with a hefty price tag on a designer website either.

For the purpose of this chapter, I'd just like to make it clear that I'm a pretty good shopper! The importance placed on value, of shopping around and not buying the first item you see, was instilled in me from a very young age. The household budget dictated that Mum had to be a bargain shopper. We'd head to the supermarket on certain days in the evening, when she knew she'd be able to buy reduced lamb chops and mince to store in the freezer. She read fashion magazines, but *always* knew someone on the market who sold pieces in similar fabrics, at a fraction of the price of those she'd loved on the glossy pages. She discovered stalls that sold last season's high-street shoes, but they'd been used in catwalk shows so were all vastly reduced. Mum was queen of the bargain. What this now means is that I am very happy to shop *everywhere*. I have absolutely zero snob value attached to stores, because I see it as a personal challenge to find the gems within them.

I get heart flutters in a junk shop, and enjoy the thrill of the chase of an online auction site. I love an out-of-town retail park as much as I love a designer outlet. I love a trip to a cavernous supermarket, with its cleverly bought home-ware, clothing ranges and variety of independent food brands. I bought lots of pieces for my wedding from an industrial hangar near my parents' home that generally sells decorations to shop owners. I get more pleasure from tracking down a classic piece on eBay and bidding, than I do walking into a department store and handing over my credit card.

I love vintage crockery, so I never ignore a charity shop. Once I spent a whole year intermittently picking up bargains to host the Christmas festivities, wherever I was shopping. I always kept one eye out for relatively inexpensive serving platters, napkins and tablecloths that would inject the spirit of Noel! I loved every minute of the search – despite the fact that it lasted for months. You can obviously go and buy everything matching from one store and get it done in a fraction of the time, but frankly, where's the fun in that? And anyway, I'm not really a matchy-matchy kind of a person!

Working in the fashion department on a daily newspaper meant that we were inundated with requests for work experience placements, with the usual caveat being: 'They'll be great – they just love shopping!' Loving shopping is all well and good, but it doesn't make a great editor. For that, you need to add in an eye and a natural instinct. Being good at shopping is a start, being a more instinctive shopper is a skill. But it's a learned skill – you can train yourself. I was a fashion assistant, then an editor for a long time. My specialist subject was the high street – and this is very much where I trained and honed the art. I did this weekly, *for years*! I developed a sixth sense about shopping which I called 'the scan'. In the same way a teacher can mark 30 books and assess each for tone and content, or a make-up artist can immediately look at a client's face and determine the perfect colours to suit them, or the way a journalist can skim read a press release and work out the exact nugget of the story, I developed a sense of where to start looking in a store when faced with an overwhelming sea of stuff.

A bit of background: my team was responsible for organising and styling all manner of photo shoots, from our own fashion stories, to celebrity photo shoots and features for other departments on the newspaper, styling 'real' people (meaning, rather than models, even though models are *obviously* real people too!). It meant that we were all experts in racing around high-street shop floors, armed with a notebook annotated with details of our models' heights, sizes, likes and dislikes, in an attempt to find pieces that would work to fit the theme for the photo shoot we had discussed with the editor. We would either arrange a store appointment through the brand's press department or head to the press team's showroom, where they always hold on to current collection samples in order to send them out to newspaper and magazine fashion teams for shoots.

It was a daily newspaper with a deadline, so we didn't have a lot of time. As a guideline, morning conference would be at around 10.30am where all the department editors would take a combined, edited list of ideas from their teams to discuss with the paper's editor. If an idea was liked, we would have a vague 'start working on this' steer by around 11.15am, with a confirmed 'right, it's happening' shout by around 12pm, after the final 'pages' meeting. We then had a few hours to organise hair, make-up, a photographer, photo studio and all the clothes, before the paper deadline at around 4pm. Oh – and we often had to write the feature too!

It was always fuelled entirely by adrenaline and an absolute cast-iron hit list of people you could rely on – from creatives to clothing brands and couriers, who had specific instructions to deliver by certain times. To this day, I genuinely think if you can work on a daily newspaper, no deadline will *ever* faze you. (The other thing is that you could give me six weeks to complete a project, but I will always leave it until the day before and have it finished before 4pm! Writing this book meant completely retraining my brain!) Anyway, back to the scan.

High-street sizing is notoriously random, depending on the store, so often we would need to make sure there were a number of variations just in case one size didn't suit on the day. Plus, we always needed extras for the rail, in case our vision didn't work (also, so nobody felt awkward or uncomfortable if they hadn't quite got their sizes right). Usually there would be a theme as to how we were to dress people for the shoot, which would have been pre-approved by the editor. It would either be colour-related or something specific, for example sequin dresses for a party feature, or white tees and denim for a simple, clean, female-focused story. We had limited time and therefore had to be strategic in our approach. Learning where each 'department' within every store sits is key to strategising your shop. Research is also crucial. You can start to compile this in your head, ultimately meaning that when you *do* shop, there's no wastage on time.

If we use Marks & Spencer as an example again, knowing that their 'Autograph' collection is the place to head if you want classic tailoring with a modern twist, or a silky tee that you can layer under a work suit, or a cashmere Breton striped knit, makes for a far more efficient shop. On the other hand, knowing that their 'Per Una' range is for more of a statement print, or for a floral with a ruffle, or an asymmetric hemline, makes it easier to decide where to immediately head upon entering the store.

H&M is another example. They have different 'departments' depending on what look you want. Their 'DIVIDED' collection is sporty and youthful, while 'L.O.G.G.' is where you'd head if you want a hoody or a band-inspired tee. Personally, 'TREND' is the area I always check out first – both in-store and online. It's the range that's a little more considered, using premium fabrics; it's where you'll find embellished jumpers, or grown-up shirts and where the majority of *those dresses* you see on Instagram appear.

Knowing where your preferred range sits in store is a way of streamlining the shopping process. It gives you a clear head, a sense of purpose and less opportunity to be distracted by all the *noise* around the rest of the store. It's about prioritising the section you know you're comfortable with and making that the first port of call. After you know what's there, you will have the confidence to check out the rest. You start to scan during this time, because you're looking at a smaller, more concentrated area. Your eye will naturally be drawn to a certain colour, or combination of colours, sitting within a merchandised area. You might be attracted to a texture or fabric that suddenly sparks a whole carnival of ideas in your head.

At this point it might be helpful to suggest that *pre-shop*, where you have done a little bit of homework about what it is you might need – so you're not randomly attacking rails *on the off chance*. Taking photographs of specific pieces you own, but are looking to match up, is helpful as a personal aide-memoire. Consider four things: what it is you need, whether it's something you will wear a lot, the price and the other pieces you could team it with. If you can't think of wearing it in combination to create three outfits with existing pieces you already own, is it worth the purchase? Is it something you could look for on a pre-loved site and find for less? Or is it something you just instantly love and know you'll get a lot of pleasure from?

Where shopping gets overwhelming is when you rush in and don't know where to begin. The scan allows you to consider micro chunks of a store, rather than a macro overview. In short, the scan is taking bite-sized sections, casting your eye over them and starting to pay attention to the pieces you have an immediate response to. When you focus, rather than meander, you start to see individual pieces, instead of a whole shop filled with noise and colour! I still do this. It's how I shop. It's why the UK's biggest high-street brands (like Marks & Spencer and John Lewis) work with me. I have had a professional relationship with their teams for many years and they trust me to 'edit' their collections and share them my way. They give me free rein of their new-in pieces; I consider each, look at new ways the prints and colours could work together, checking to see whether there is one stand-out 'hero' piece that I just know will be popular – and then I showcase how I'd wear them on my social media.

And I tell you, the scan is a great skill to have when you're wandering aimlessly around a shop or scrolling mind-lessly on an app. Being able to instantly work out the colours and styles that will suit you means you cut to the chase, get down to the nitty-gritty and sniff out those pieces that are perfect for you to try. You'll save hours of physical and emotional labour! If you want to push yourself a little further out of your clothing comfort zone, just take it one piece at a time. For example, if you've gone shopping with an idea in your head to find an edgy, all-black outfit, but your comfort zone is florals, then scan for one piece that might work to give a sense of this look, without the need to immediately wear it head to toe. It could be a leather jacket, which gives a nod to the style you like and also has the effect of working to 'toughen up' those already existing floral pieces in your wardrobe. Pairing the new piece with your comfort pieces for a while will allow you to build up the confidence to add that 'edge' you want. Then perhaps, next time, you could look for a pair of biker-style ankle boots, again that would work with your florals. Conversely, if your vibe is already on the grungier side, but you'd like to start including a splash more colour into your wardrobe, scan for a piece that will straddle that line between comfort and creativity. Start off small: a tee shirt with a splash of colour or a pair of earrings, even a new, brighter shade of lipstick will all help to build that confidence. Once you feel comfortable with the baby step you take, you can gradually take a few more.

If you're drawn to something, there is a reason for that – and if it doesn't immediately seem like it would work, it's always worth holding it up and appraising for a couple of minutes to see whether there are any ways of altering it slightly to make it better suit you.

ADD AN ACCESSORY

Accessories are the perfect way to make an outfit truly yours. For example, I never keep hold of the belts that come with dresses, skirts or trousers. Generally, they're not exciting – they keep a look quite 'quiet' and you could definitely do better to create something more individual. While you're scanning, bear this in mind, because you may be attracted to a piece but not the belt. It doesn't matter because you can change it. Belts are a key part of creating a unique look. They can change the proportions of your body, by cinching and defining a waist, or readjusting where you'd like to draw attention to the idea of a waist. The way you wear your belt doesn't just add interest to an outfit. Play around with where it sits, because pushing a thicker belt further down (instead of on a natural waist) can hide unsightly seams, as well as avoid fabric puffing out around the stomach area. A thinner belt will give you the illusion of a short body and longer legs, while a wide belt will give you the appearance of a longer body and shorter legs.

Belts can update a dress to create a more contemporary outfit. They can adjust a shape of dress that might make you feel too 'girly', when actually you'd prefer to look a little more 'edgy'. By this I mean playing around with the conventions of a particular piece. So traditionally, you might team your floral dress with a smart pair of court shoes, accessorised to pick out one of the colours within the print. Now, there is absolutely nothing wrong with that (no right or wrong, remember!), but sometimes you might not want to rock a particularly feminine outfit from head to toe. You may fancy taking the dress and toughening it up a little with a studded or heavy gilt-style belt.

While you're scanning, it's worth looking at ways to use belts in unconventional ways too – for example, when wearing a one-colour, bright dress beneath a simple, boyfriend-style knee-length coat in a contrast colour, using a printed belt featuring the colour of the dress *over* the top of the coat (to close it) will pull the look together. The eye will form a 'match' between the two colours, while that combination *plus* the contrast-colour coat will add a splash of your personality.

Sometimes the simplest of accessories – be it a belt or a pair of earrings – can marry a combination of pieces that on first appearance shouldn't have a relationship with each other. Vintage belts, or even scarves, are brilliant replacements for belts that come with an item. I always keep my eye out for woven styles or printed sashes or even interesting leather styles with gold hardware. On the high street, Zara, Essentiel Antwerp and Marks & Spencer often have interesting belts. They're definitely a great way to add an individual sparkle to your look and it's worth building up a collection of favourites.

Change up your laces in those lace-up boots – swap the standard boring black for gorgeous Liberty print, neon fabric or even ribbons. Keep a belt that came with a dress (that you replaced!) to wear around a ponytail. Think about replacing the buttons on something. It's about looking at pieces in an unconventional way and considering how else they could be used in a way that feels comfortable to you.

The lowdown on hosiery

Another question I am often asked is whether you can wear tights with evening shoes. Most of us – particularly as we get older – are not about that bare-legged life *at all* when the weather drops below freezing, nor are we Anna Wintour, editor of US *Vogue*, who *never* wears them, but does have a car waiting for her at most places she attends! There may be occasions when you have an event, but *need* to wear tights. There are a few ways of looking at this style conundrum, but the answer, in short, is yes, you can. As a general rule of thumb, I tend to match the colour of my tights to the colour of my shoes – so black shoes = black tights, navy ankle boots = navy tights. It's just a very simple way of dressing, looks good and requires next to no thinking. The most popular choice of tights is black – and thick, black opaque tights work best with a black, closed-toe shoe or boot.

If you have an event to go to and want to wear an open-toed stiletto shoe, I would always suggest a skin-coloured sheer, a very sheer pattern – such as a spot – or a fishnet tight. Because they are sheer, they also work well with most shoe styles – from strappy stilettos and lace-up brogues, through to chunkier boots teamed with dresses. Black sheers do tend to work better with black or dark-hued shoes, rather than, say, a metallic or coloured shoe, simply because the contrast between the two is too stark. Stiletto shoes just don't tend to work well with opaque tights; the proportions are slightly off (it all looks too 'heavy') and it can make the whole outfit look a little old-fashioned. A more modern approach is to wear a platform open-toe shoe or a simple ankle-strap, open-toe thin-heeled shoe, which looks chic worn with a contrast (or same-coloured) pair of tights, as it provides some 'weight' to your outfit and pretty much works with most styles.

If your shoe colour is lighter – say, for example, a neutral beige – choose a skin-coloured sheer, either plain or with a slight pattern on it. I love Heist Studio's 'Nude' tights, which come in seven representative shades. They're consistently raved about as the best tights out there and, thanks to a high thread count, they're soft and they keep their shape. Also, there isn't a central seam (it's under the foot), so they don't snag against your toenails. They're more expensive, but look after them and they're a great investment.

Bright-coloured opaque tights, on the other hand, are a statement, but can look amazing with the right outfit – and they keep you warm. A good tip is to choose your colour by *either* matching it to your shoe *or* picking it out of your outfit. Choose the base colour of your skirt or dress, or a predominant shade within the print of that item. That way, the eye connects the two shades and the whole look is seamless. This is why it can appear a bit jarring if you wear a dark opaque tight with a lighter shoe, because the eye can't connect the colours anywhere and the contrast is too stark. A top tip: if black tights are too heavy for an outfit you're wearing, but sheer won't cut the mustard, choose a burgundy or maroon pair of opaques, which flatter every skin tone.

Trouser lovers can obviously stick a pair of tights on underneath their trousers, either for warmth or for those all-important couple of inches flashed at ankle level. This is a great idea if you love the cropped, wide-leg ankle-length trousers that are currently fashionable, but can't stand the idea of going with a bare ankle in the middle of winter. But, you don't need to resort to pop socks! There is the option – if you want to make a real style statement – to opt for the *disco sock*! The disco sock is generally ankle height, contains a smattering of lurex thread, or glitter, or fishnet, and can be worn with flat shoes – and, if you're feeling party-ready, heels. These are posh socks, not your common or garden black cotton basics! But they don't cost posh prices, because places like COS, & Other Stories and

Topshop are great with their disco socks and are definitely worth a look. You'll either love them or hate them – but, if you fancy giving them a go, you could start off with something simple, such as teaming a pair with a trouser suit and lace-up brogues for the office, or with jeans, sweatshirt and trainers for a casual look. Starting off small builds up your confidence – and then one day you may well think 'Tonight's the night for the heels and the disco socks!' Your outfit, your rules.

Just add jewellery

Jewellery is probably the most transformative of all accessories. By just changing the kind of jewellery you wear with a simple dress, for example, you can go from day to night. If money is tight, but you have something in the diary that requires a bit of effort being made, choose something simple, then add personality with jewellery. Through your choice of accessories, you make the whole look uniquely yours. And it doesn't have to be expensive; you can find one-off pieces in junk shops, or in department store concessions, or even the supermarket. You might already have an amazing dress that you once spent a fortune on, but it just needs a bit of a facelift to re-wear for a function – consider a piece of jewellery. Clusters of hand-me-down brooches on a simple jacket, stacks of beaded bangles bought over many years of holiday market shopping, a curated ear lobe (multiple, precious metal piercings on your ears) all help to create that individual look. Often, it's the mix of pieces that makes an outfit most interesting.

SHOPPING: THEN AND NOW

If you put something on and you *feel* something about it – if you feel amazing and expensive and chic – you will project that feeling. If you put something on and you feel casual, a bit scruffy and as though you'd hate to bump into anyone you know, you will project that feeling. It's about treating clothes – and yourself – with respect, regardless of their cost. Cut, colour and fabric are your three buzzwords. If it's a classic you can wear it with lots of different things, whereas if it's just a fashion-piece, it tends to only go with certain things. And remember, particularly if you're shopping for vintage or in the sales, there are a few garments to always keep a look out for. One-button blazers are *always* chic. In fact, you just can't go wrong with smart tailoring; buttonless coats, where they don't fasten and just hang, are also a great addition to every wardrobe. The main thing to keep in mind is to shop for what suits you. Be inspired by trends, but do it your way.

Of course, the entire experience of shopping has changed drastically since I started working in fashion back in the early noughties. While once we may have spent the day mooching with friends, now we are more likely to do it all online and go for experience days with pals instead. I know I would prefer to meet up for a lovely lunch and leave the shopping until the evening, when I can scroll and buy anything I might need or want on an app. Traditional retail is an industry that is being forced to change with the times. The numbers of physical stores on the high street are reducing, with research stating that the amount of empty shops on the UK high street is now just over 10 per cent – the highest level since 2015. The same research suggests that the top 150 UK retailers have 20 per cent more shop space now than they need or, crucially, that they can afford to run. Why? Because customers are now spending one in every five pounds online – and if businesses are seeing 20 per cent fewer sales on the shop floor as well as their fixed costs rising, then profit margins will naturally be squeezed.

The pleasures of a traditional shopping day out have simply drained away. Having a mediocre customer experience trailing from one chain to the next just doesn't pull in the punters in the same way it once did. There's more competition for your time and money. And mediocre is exactly the word for the experience it has become. Stores might try: they might add in nail bars and cupcake stations and 'Instagram-style' photo booths to lure in the shopper, but standards of customer service have slipped. Other financial pressures have taken precedence over the importance of management ensuring their teams are up to standard.

That's not to do all retail staff a disservice though; there are plenty of good ones out there who respect their customers and find a balance between the commercial goals of the business and the happiness of the client. It should also be made clear that there are many different types of 'shop' too, from market stalls and high-street precincts, to shopping centres, out-of-town retail parks and uber-malls. Each plays a different role in its geographical location – so the shops that are important for a country village share a different relationship to people living in a large city, for example. What happens to these areas as the stores close down has different costs attached depending on their purpose.

To me, as someone whose career was based entirely on the high street, it's clear that the whole shopping experience has to be just that. An experiential one, offering something the online store simply can't; pop-up events, masterclasses, servicing the niches of the brand and their customer database and building on that community *within* the community. Smaller stores need to up the ante on 'service', with expert advice and help, meaning customers will trust and return.

It used to be that if your town didn't have a Marks & Spencer or a Starbucks, it was somehow failing. But the last time I got excited about a new store opening was when a charity venture for a local hospice created a vintage store, with an edited collection of clothing and interiors. They created a real vibe, with industrial brickwork walls and staff with an eye for merchandising, upcycled scaffolding pipes and rustic wooden floors. It was packed. It was exciting. It was different. If we're all naturally turning more and more to our phones for both our shopping and our social life, there needs to be a way of getting our attention back. Perhaps, after a century-long cloning of the Great British High Street, it wouldn't be a *terrible* idea if local towns looked to create more spaces like this – and rather than rely totally on retail, play upon their individual local industries, produce, crafts and heritage for inspiration in creating new, independent stores, event centres and experiential pop-ups, rather than the homogenised high streets of old.

The all-powerful, omnipresent online is another animal. It's a 24/7 beast and that means shopping is available at the tap of an app, whenever you want. Where standalone stores simply can't physically contain *all* the stock, online works because entire ranges are already uploaded and ready to go. As long as the logistics work – next-day delivery, delivery choices, email notifications and free returns – it's a very stress-free experience for the customer. And, if you like a particular shop, there's a way to scan online too. For me, this is about building a relationship with the 'new-in' sections of a website. With my favourite high-street stores, I check in with their new-in regularly. It allows me to get a sense of what trends they're pushing, to look at colour ideas and also to get a sense of how often they're refreshing their stock.

Zara is a really good example of a brand that has created a hugely successful business model by learning *exactly* how its customers shop. Firstly, it works with a low level of inventory – meaning it only makes what it knows it can sell. Zara refreshes its stock both online and in-store twice a week (usually on a Monday and Thursday, depending on where you are), which ensures customers are constantly inspired to purchase (it also means 9.30am on those days are the times to try to get your size, but also that a Saturday is a bad time to shop there!). Zara has embraced algorithms and knows what sells well. This means that it updates versions of the same bestselling pieces throughout the season. So even if you miss out on something that sold out quickly, the designers will quickly turn around a new colour or version within weeks. (However, if you did miss out on something, do keep checking in with the pre-loved websites I mentioned earlier in the book – see page 48. Depop is one that's great for high-street buys.)

Most brand websites now offer 'inspiration' tabs as part

of their online customer experience, adding in a touch of 'aspirational lifestyle' to an otherwise transaction-only experience. & Other Stories, a Swedish store from the same stable as H&M, COS, ARKET, Monki and Weekday, even has a 'Most Wanted' tab on its site, showing the bestselling pieces from its collection. Clever . . . but it can create the anxiety of needing it now. Don't let the sense of others buying an item mean that you have to have it as well! Consider how you'll wear it and what you'll wear it with first.

Online superstore ASOS has fresh deliveries every day, so keeping an eye on the new-in would be a full-time job. For this kind of site – where, if I'm honest, as a woman in her forties, I'm not the target demographic – it's about making friends with your filters in order to find a gem or three. Because, despite the brand not necessarily targeting me, there are pieces that I love. As with auction sites such as eBay, there are ways of finding things without losing your mind (and the feeling in your fingers) as you scroll. On ASOS, I always filter down to the brands (choose 'Brands' from the menu choice). For example, I know that I like ASOS Design in their own brands and & Other Stories, Whistles and Sister Jane in their bought-in brands. If I don't want to scroll everything within that 'department', I refine further to a specific item, selecting 'Product type' and then further refine by 'Size'.

Often, as with shopping IRL (In Real Life), online stores offer too much choice – and if you're just 'window/screen shopping', it's overwhelming. Have a strong idea in mind of what it is you're after before you even start – and stay focused on that particular product, style or colour. Otherwise, if you have the time, by all means knock yourself out and scroll through every new-in item! Remember, too, most items saved in your basket will stay there for weeks, or at least until the product sells out. So, if you're not in the mood right there and then, leave it in your basket and return to it when you are – or when you've been paid. I'm also a big fan of the 'saved item' function, where you can keep a virtual wish list of pieces saved in your account. This is a really useful one for ASOS, because even if something has sold out, if the size you want is saved within your wish list, you will be notified if one is returned.

SCANNING FOR VINTAGE

Give me a second-hand store or a vintage auction and I am like the proverbial pig in muck. Part of my honeymoon was based around a trip to L'Isle sur la Sorgue, so we could visit one of France's largest brocante (second-hand market) fairs (I say 'we' . . . I think we all know that's not strictly true). eBay, for me, is uncharted brocante territory. One man's trash is another man's treasure and all that. If I have a specific thing to track down, I could spend *hours* on the site. Searching on eBay depends on many factors: what your budget is, whether you're aware of the current 'best price' for your searched-for item and how you use the search function itself.

On eBay, finding the bargains is *all* about the search terms. I tracked down a Jaeger dress I had been looking for since 2005, but couldn't afford then. Wanting to find it over a decade later, I saved 'Jaeger boutique dress' and the size I wanted in a 'follow this search' setting. Regularly searched-for items can be saved by entering the item you're interested in, pressing enter and then clicking on the 'follow this search' text that appears at the top. This means your homepage will show anything that relates to your item quest when it comes up. If you want to be alerted as soon as there's a new listing ('Yes! Tell me when it comes up!'), simply check the 'email me new items that match this interest' button.

You have to be patient. I kept checking for this particular dress over a period of a few years. Then finally, *finally*, there it was – a 15-year search came to fruition! The seller had just listed it, but I took a punt and asked if she would consider a buy-it-now price (all is fair in love and fashion), which – as no one else had bid on it – she did. We agreed to a price over eBay messages and I bought it. The deal was done.

Being specific is crucial. My mum and dad own a Parker Knoll wing back chair that has been re-covered – in my lifetime – around five times. I love it, it reminds me of my grandma sitting in it when she came round for Sunday lunch or at Christmas; it was her chair. As a grown-up (apparently), living in my own home, I wanted my own version. I was also inspired by my friend who had found one at an antiques fair and had it reupholstered in the coolest citrus felt. I wanted one for my living room, to give it a bit of modern-day granny chic. But I didn't want to scroll through thousands of 'vintage sofas' as I knew the specific style I was after. If you're searching for more than one thing, you can use brackets and commas to separate. So, for example, if you wanted a Parker Knoll style wing back sofa too, you could search for (wing back, Parker Knoll, sofa). Adding a minus sign immediately before a word (with no space) acts as a 'not operator', so searching for (wing back sofa -chair) will ignore any listings that specify 'chair' in the title. For fashion just replace the furniture aspect of my above example with the clothing item you're hankering after, for example 'vintage black velvet blazer -coat'. I actually started a secret Pinterest board of the fashion pieces I couldn't afford or had never found – and kept referring back to it periodically to try to see whether I could track down any pre-loved versions of them.

One of the pieces I absolutely loved, but would never have been able to justify buying at full price, was a Max Mara 101801 Icon coat – slouchy, yet feminine, wool and cashmere, untouched in design since its launch in 1981. An absolute steal at around £2000 brand new! And yet I had been inspired to revisit the search after spotting several people I follow on Instagram wearing them. I decided now was the time for me to try again with a slightly more affordable (in my world) version. I was as specific as possible on eBay, checking in the actual coat details, the fact I wanted a vintage version and the size I was after. Again, after a few months of activity, a couple of lovely styles came up – but then one I *really* loved appeared. It had quite a few bids active on it already, so making a buy-it-now offer wouldn't be allowed. (Side note: if you like the look of something, but aren't that impressed by the images, email the seller and ask for more detailed shots and imagery. If they're serious sellers, they will be happy to help.)

Anyway, back to the Max Mara coat. I entered my absolute maximum bid (on eBay, it doesn't automatically jump to that maximum, but rather keeps incrementally going up if another bidder competes against you) and waited. I had decided that if it was meant to be mine, it would, but my maximum was the absolute maximum and I wasn't going to get all over-excited and panic-press a higher bid. And I won! It was my maximum bid – and still a couple of hundred pounds – but a thrill nonetheless to finally win a coat I'd been after for years.

There is very little in this world more satisfying than tracking down that item you've wanted for ages – at a vastly reduced price. In this swipe-and-buy-immediately culture that social media has created, I feel we've lost that sense of shopping success. I spent my teen years (way before the Internet!) clutching ripped-out pages of magazines and trailing around high-street stores to see if they stocked specific pieces. I watched TV shows where characters wore clothes that inspired me, and I made pilgrimages to second-hand stores to find similar. It was the thrill of the chase, the joy of spotting things in magazines and trying to scan for them when I was next out shopping – and I feel that has been lost somewhat, because now everything is so widely available.

Perhaps we need to go back to that mindset – where we open our eyes to the possibilities of broadly shopping, rather than the tunnel-vision shuttle runs to the supermarket, or Saturday morning trips to the retail park. Instead of online-only, venture to new, local towns and check out their independent stores and charity shops. Use the Internet to research great vintage shops within a 20-mile radius or designer discount outlets. Make a day of it. Find yourself a great pub for lunch or a lovely café for a coffee. Make shopping a real pleasure, not a chore. Just find your happy way of doing it.

FIVE POINTS TO TAKE AWAY

1. View every store, charity shop and market as a potential opportunity to find a clothing gem. Creating your own look is about telling a story and that can come from anywhere.

2. You can hone your shopping skills to 'zone out' all the noise and focus in on the pieces you're instantly attracted to.

3. Research is key to being a good shopper – know what it is you want to look for and learn which parts of the store are best for that. Online, find out the days your favourite brands add their new-in pieces.

4. Consider four things when you find something you like: Do you need it? Will you wear it a lot? Is the price right? What else could you wear it with? If you can't think of wearing it in combination to create three outfits with existing pieces you already own, is it worth the purchase?

5. If you want to push yourself a little further out of your clothing comfort zone, just take it one piece at a time. Once you feel comfortable with the baby step you take, you can gradually take a few more.

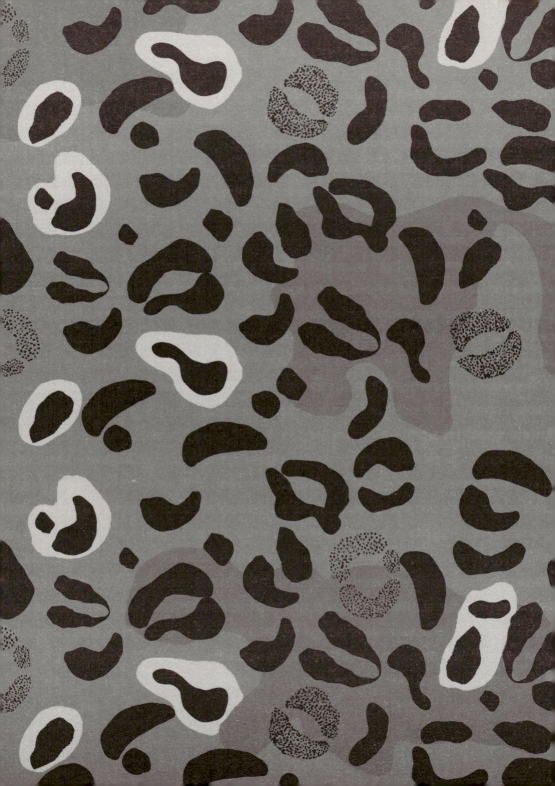

The Style Tricks You Do Need to Know

CHAPTER SEVEN

THE STYLE TRICKS YOU *DO* NEED TO KNOW

It's a new era in fashion – there are no rules. It's all about the individual and personal style, wearing high-end, low-end, classic labels, and up-and-coming designers all together.
—Alexander McQueen

Fashion 'rules' have previously sent us the message that in order to look good, we need to create the 'perfect' silhouette by whatever means. Generally, this involves 'fooling the eye' with the clothing choices you make. It involves wearing body-contorting underclothes beneath; huge pants that pull in your stomach and thighs; bras that push up, or smooth down, or reduce.

For a long time, I did just that. I wrote about it, I styled people that way, I bought the *actual* tee shirt – and then I asked myself, 'Why?' *Who* decided that women have to fit into one specific size mould? And anyway, now if I'm feeling a bit bloated or uncomfortably premenstrual, I'll just wear a looser shape – I don't want to force myself into a pair of control pants. We all come in different shapes and sizes, with each and every one of us looking different – naked or dressed. It is a tiring narrative – and more than that, it is reductive – to assume that there are categories of body shape in this world and everyone who happens to fall into one of them can look 'good' if they all follow the same rules.

Google 'body shape rules' online and you are hit with page after page after *page* of websites all claiming to teach the best way of dressing for your triangular, pear, hourglass, apple, athletic, straight-up-and-down or petite body. I'm talking about the articles that liken women's bodies to fruit before suggesting what we should or shouldn't wear, based on which fruit or other inanimate object our bodies resemble. You've all read it before (I mean, I probably *wrote* it before); things like, 'If you're a pear, don't wear pencil skirts or horizontal stripes', 'If you're straight up and down, wear a push-up bra and a wide belt', 'If you're an apple, never wear shorts'.

While researching this book, I looked back at newspaper and magazine articles discussing body shape dressing (yes, including my own!) and was slightly horrified by the 'advice' dispensed. This one, from 2016, stuck in my mind because I couldn't quite believe that – so recently – it was deemed OK to tell women that if they are hourglass they should 'avoid swamping in tents'; that, if you have boobs and a bum, you 'need to nip in at the waist'; and, if you are blessed with a chest, you shouldn't wear something without a waist as 'it will make you look enormous'. That piece was written by a woman – clearly 'trying' to offer what she considered honest, practical, realistic advice. But look at the amount of negative words she uses in this paragraph: avoid, swamping, tents, need and enormous. There are so many things to unpick here. It's also highlighting a real issue with perceptions within fashion – that it's a 'them and us' situation. 'They' are the ones who have the shapes we see on a catwalk, 'us' are the rest – with boobs and thighs and bums that 'need fixing' or 'disguising' in order to look more like 'them'.

What real purpose do body shape guides serve, other than making us feel really bad about ourselves? They assign us all useless, potentially damaging labels based on fruit or other random objects, they lump women's bodies into a handful of categories, they assign those categories rigid rules for dressing and they make us all – no matter what shape we are – feel weird and self-conscious about our size. To me, being truly confident in your style – and in your body – means being happy as well as healthy.

Swimsuit guides have always been the worst kind of anti-female propaganda – and, certainly for me, created years of anxiety about actually putting one on and baring my thighs to the world, or at least the people around the pool. Magazines have done it for years – showing paparazzi shots of celebrities on the beach, with headlines speculating about their 'beach-ready' bodies, whether they've lost weight or, shock horror, put weight on. Ignore the *actual* narrative. Never mind the fact that they may be having fun with their family, unaware of the camera lens zooming in, ready to take photos that will be published alongside an article pulling apart their choice of swimwear, their thighs and their lack of make-up.

I remember seeing one particular swimwear guide which used images of 'real women' they had taken on the beach. One very happy image of a lady in a strapless bikini top and matching bottoms had a headline saying 'WRONG!' with a caption explaining how she shouldn't wear that style of bikini top because she had small breasts. Next to it was an image of a push-up bikini top with the word 'RIGHT!' above it. Hang on, what was 'wrong' about it in the first place? The fact she happened to have small boobs and dared to wear a bandeau top? The same article suggested that no one over a size 14 should ever wear a bikini, only ever a one-piece.

Body shape guides feed into the insecurities laid down by years and years of female style 'advice' – and to try to get us to buy whatever the magazine agenda is. Now I'm definitely not here to say certain ways of dressing are 'wrong'. I'm not even here to say don't follow those 'rules'. I don't agree with many of them, but if they work for you and you feel happier about dressing to some kind of structure, then go for it. Just please remember that their message is restrictive. Dressing well is so much about yourself and how you feel in the clothes you choose, not whether you happen to be built in the same vague shape as a piece of fruit.

Fashion editors are hired because they have a talent and an instinct for pairing shapes, colours and textures together. They can create amazing visuals to help inspire and offer suggestions. What should *really* be out of fashion is prescribing outdated, anti-feminist notions wrapped up as 'life rules'. Really, *you* are the only fashion authority you need to listen to. Sure, you can appreciate the ideas of others, but your gut instinct and response to clothes are all you need. What I hope this book does is give you a bit of confidence. I'd love it if it could help get you to a point where you can block out that kind of historical style noise and not only accept yourself, as you are right now, but find some pretty amazing outfits along the way to *truly* reflect who you are.

What I *do* want to share is some practical advice for dressing – so rather than the structure being based upon fruit-based body shapes (eye-roll), it will offer clear guidance on how you can make the most of your outfits. There are a couple of tricks that will *always* work to make clothes look as good as they can. Not *you*, not *your body*, just your clothes.

UNDERSTANDING PROPORTION

The first of these is proportion. Now I don't mean – as discussed earlier – proportions to cheat the eye, disguise your shape and proportions of your body. I'm talking about the proportions of clothing that will work best together to create a killer outfit. Working out the proportions that best work for you will make shopping *and* dressing easier. You'll have a greater understanding of the shapes to buy to wear with your existing clothes and also those that would make great investments. Whenever I am dressing someone, be it a model or myself, the first thing I look at are proportions. Sizes and numbers don't really matter, but if you want an outfit to have balance and power, proportions definitely do. Fashion – particularly fashion seen in magazine editorials – often plays quite dramatically with proportions, but you can modify this (or recreate it if you fancy an edgier look!) to suit your own personal style.

Lines are an easier way to try to explain, because your eye and mind will always follow a line. So, if you're wearing a Breton top, for example, the eye will follow the lines width-wise. If you're wearing a V-neck top and a longer line coat, the eye will be drawn down, creating more of a lengthening visual. In order to create a proportional look for you, you need to know the shape you want to create. And always,

always focus on the positives. If you focus on the parts you don't like, then the whole process starts from a negative mindset. Plus, if you focus on the positives then the negative stuff will sort of disappear. You absolutely *can* dress in whatever you like, no matter if it's 'right' or 'wrong' for your shape. But if you feel like nothing you put on makes you look the way you want, then perhaps thinking about proportions and lines can change that.

Coat lengths and hemlines

OK, so let's start. First up, coat lengths. For me, a coat works best if the hemline beneath it (i.e. your skirt or dress) doesn't show by more than a couple of centimetres. It sends the proportions of the rest of your outfit all off. My advice would be pretty simple: try to match the hemline of your dress or skirt to the hemline of your coat. So, if you're wearing a midi skirt (calf- or ankle-length), a knee-length coat wouldn't look as good as if you wear it with a calf- or ankle-length coat. There's a mismatch of lengths and it will make the proportions of your outfit look a bit 'off'. The same goes for wearing a miniskirt with a much longer coat – because the amount of leg on show in proportion to your skirt and coat will be off balance.

There is an exception: a trench coat – which is generally midi-length – looks great worn over maxi-length skirts. The whole leg is covered by material anyway, so the proportions work. If you want to wear your skirt or dress with a blazer or a leather jacket that hits the waist, you don't need to worry about the hemlines matching. Waist-length styles work proportionally with everything. Trousers are an exception – in that knee-length coats will work proportionally, as will waist-length jackets and even maxi-length coats. Again, though, it's important to consider the proportions. Wide-leg trousers that flare out from the thighs will work best with shorter coats or jackets that hit the waist as they will balance the look. (Side note: wide-leg trousers and oversized jumpers work, but stick to flat or chunky shoes because then the proportions are balanced.) Heels will give the impression of too much width up top, balancing on precarious-looking, spiky heels, and it will look as though you'll topple over! Grounding this kind of outfit with chunkier flats or trainers is the way to keep things proportional. Slim-fit trousers can work with most coat shapes, so you can play around with proportions. You might fancy an androgynous look and go for a leather biker jacket, a cropped aviator coat or even a straight-up-and-down knee-length boyfriend style. Or you may want to play around a bit and choose a slightly more oversized coat, which still accounts for the proportions of your outfit.

Skirting around

There's currently a trend for a midi-length skirt (who am I kidding? I always *love* a midi!), but when I share an image of them on Instagram, I always have messages from people saying they feel frumpy and aren't sure how to wear them 'properly'. Again, no rules – just best-practice proportion advice. For pleated styles, fabric is a big consideration. Floatier, lightweight fabrics do look more flattering if you have curvier hips, like me. I tend to avoid heavier fabrics such as thick cotton or velvet as they add to the width and can throw off proportions even more. But satin, tulle and light, summer-weight cotton hang and move more fluidly, plus they have way more pairing options.

Crew-neck jumpers (or sweatshirts if you want to have a go at making a fancy skirt less, well, fancy) work beautifully, because proportionally they hit the waist and allow the width of the skirt be the star of the show. There's nothing that jars or tries to 'compete'. Simple camisoles tucked into the skirt (in a similar fabric to the skirt), worn with a blazer is another outfit idea for your skirt. Or, if you don't like the idea of wearing a camisole on its own, you could layer it over a long- or short-sleeved tee shirt. Look for styles that aren't your classic thicker cottons – so silks or sheer cotton or jersey would work best layered underneath another top. Then the whole outfit is fluid and doesn't look too 'stiff'.

You definitely don't need to listen to old style rules about having one fitted separate and one flowing, because a loose, oversized knit jumper works beautifully with a silky midi skirt. You could try teaming with knee-high fabric boots in a similar colour to the skirt, or tonally coloured tights and open-toe, seventies-style platform heels. Heels would work best with this kind of outfit, simply because the height balances out the width and size of the jumper and avoids a 'fabric overload' situation.

Style shape-shifting

You may want to try to recreate a completely different shape to the one you're born with using clothes. And that's fine – fashion editorials have always played with the appearance of proportion – so here's where playing with lines and proportion comes in handy. You may fancy trying a blouse or jumper with huge, blouson sleeves paired with a slim-fit pencil skirt, to give a sort of inverted triangle shape. Or try fitted, ankle-length trousers with an oversized cocoon-style coat. Try layering a long kimono-style jacket over a pair of cigarette pants and a white shirt, or a midi-length shirt dress over a pair of wide-leg trousers. Looser tops will work best proportionally with slim trousers (and if your top is tunic- or midi-length, keep the trousers cropped at the ankle), while wide-leg trousers will work best proportionally with a more fitted top.

You may feel self-conscious about your boobs and prefer to find fewer cleavage-focused ways of dressing. Ruffles, frills and low-cut tops are all well-documented breast-enhancers, meaning they *will* attract attention! So consider other combinations where the outfit is the focus, rather than just the top half. If you want to play around with ruffles, for example, try wearing something with them on the sleeve or where the hem of a top meets the waistband. Choose a pocket-free shirt, rather than one with patch pockets that may highlight your boobs. You can wear a polo neck, but think about layering a scoop or V-neck top over it in a different colour or pattern, as the combination of necklines will kind of 'confuse the eye' and make it difficult to focus entirely on your chest.

If you're bottom-heavy, you may feel self-conscious wearing tight-fitting trousers or skirts, but really, you shouldn't, it's simply about getting the proportions right. Wide-leg trousers are a classic shape, because they fall beautifully from the waist. I like wearing a slightly cropped pair, with a heeled ankle boot in the same colour that hits just under the hem of the trouser – the continuation of the same colour gives a more streamlined look, while the shape of the cropped trousers and boots adds interest. Similarly, a wide-leg trouser that 'breaks' on top of a flat lace-up shoe or trainer works well with a slouchy knit, tucked slightly into the waistband. Or with a blouse tucked in, but pulled out a little around the waistband, worn with a blazer. An A-line skirt that flares out over your bum works well with pretty much any kind of top you fancy teaming it with, while pleated or bias-cut skirt styles could add volume and distort the proportions of your outfit. Don't give up on trying fitted pencil skirt styles though, as often curves look fabulous and sexy in them. Consider the fabric choice for structure – leather would look brilliant worn with a crew neck and slouchy blazer, or team a satin pencil with a longer length, oversized knit.

If you're petite, proportions are very important. Cropped, fitted trousers are a great style to wear as they give a little flash of ankle which gives a sense of 'length'. Wearing an on-the-knee skirt will keep things balanced – if it's full and fabric-heavy, balance this on your top half with a simple shape, for example a tee shirt and fitted jacket. If it's a pencil shape, try pairing with a blouse that's full of detail – a romantic ruffled collar situation, or blouson sleeve blouse with a statement necklace. You don't need to stick to heels if you're petite – unless you want to, of course – but keeping colour continuity with your shoe + bottom-half choice does work best.

PATTERN PLAY

Proportions don't just have to relate to shape – they can play with pattern too. One of my all-time favourites is a stripe – which I do think plays well with most other patterns in a wardrobe – paired with another stripe. A narrow striped tee, worn with a contrast direction striped skirt, or even a pair of trousers with a wider print, works. You could look at wearing a ditsy (small) floral printed blouse with a much larger floral printed skirt. They could even be completely contrasting prints, but as we've already mentioned, keeping at least two of the colours similar will connect them together (see page 72). It keeps the narrative going between the two pieces and gives your outfit a more thought-through look.

Wearing with a belt will emphasise the idea that they're separates, while leaving a belt off will make it look more like a dress. Sometimes it might give you more confidence to break up the print a little – so the belt may help. Or even adding in a block colour in the form of a jacket or longer coat might dilute it to a level with which you're happier. However, putting prints together in this way needn't be showy or an exercise in drawing attention to yourself. It probably used to be – or as a 'disguise' for curves – but actually there's something incredibly chic about getting to grips with a pattern or three. They can really help you feel excited about clothes.

If you already follow me on social media (hello!), you'll know that I am unapologetic about my love of colour and pattern. For me it's a real energiser – when you're feeling a bit down, or the day is grey and miserable, you can actually alter the way you're feeling, simply by getting dressed. But you don't need to turn yourself into a children's TV presenter or, heaven forbid, a clown, by piling on the clashing prints and bright colours – you can dilute, change and mix it up in a way that suits you.

When you can print clash
- When the pieces you want to wear share one or more common colours.
- When the pieces you want to wear share similar tones of the same colour family.
- When you just want to wear those two pieces and own it.

The joy of three

At this point I'd like to bring in my 'trio tip'. It's a simple one but it does bring a certain clarity to the possible overwhelm of the print clash. If you fancy trying print or colour, but aren't sure where to start, then think about your outfit's components in terms of three. I also use this as a guide when

I decorate a room, by the way – it's a good one to get the balance right. Take a main piece – for the sake of an example, let's suggest it's a bright pink and orange printed skirt, with a hint of white in the pattern too. Immediately you can dissect that skirt to three main colours: the base pink, the highlight orange and white. Overall, the predominant colour is pink. Styling wise, I would mix in a striped top with a white base and a pink stripe. I would leave those two pieces having a conversation, so I wouldn't throw in another print, but rather pick out plain pieces in the accent colours, for example a plain white blazer and a pair of orange heels. Within the context of the outfit, you've only used three colours, but you've done so in a way that keeps it all interesting.

Let's take another example, just to make sure it's clear and I'm not overcomplicating. You've picked out a V-neck, loose-fit, navy blue floral printed dress. It has short sleeves. The base colour is navy, but the print has a bit of green, white and brown in it too. It's a cooler day, but you still want to wear it, so you pull out a floral polo neck which you want to layer underneath the dress. The print is different and much smaller proportionally than the one on the dress, but it contains all of the same colours. It has a base colour of white, with a navy and brown print. Even if the print is different, it doesn't matter, because your eye will connect up the colours that are the same. Layer your long-sleeved polo neck under your short-sleeved dress (both for warmth and for interest) and then add in your third piece (trio tip!). For this I would suggest picking out the green colour of the dress and wearing this in a pair of boots or a coat. That way your rule of three would be the two prints, plus the highlight colour.

In terms of interiors, I put rooms together in the same way I put an outfit together: one predominant shade that will be the main focus, plus two accent colours. In our living room, for example, I've used a rich blue shade on the walls and painted bookshelves (it's Juniper Ash by Little Greene – and if I had a pound for every time someone has asked me on social media . . . !). Our sofa is in a deeper shade of navy blue, which tones with the blue of the wall, and I have kept a lot of the prints of the cushions in similar blue tones. However, our staircase – which you can see from the living room – has a runner in a vibrant, grass green colour. So, I connected the spaces together visually with the inclusion in the living room of a second-hand Dutch cupboard I found on eBay, painted in the same green as the staircase.

This then becomes the second most predominant colour in the room (forget the rules, blue and green should *always* be seen!) and it gave me more ideas for adding in accessories, including cushions containing the same green, on their own, within a pattern with the blue – and with room softeners such as large plants. I also re-covered two second-hand armchairs in a tropical green fabric, which ties together visually with the cupboard and the stairs. The final accent colour, brought in on cushion patterns, plain cushions and some artwork, is a sunshine yellow. The colours all work together in nature – and I love the combination in my own home. But pattern clashing aside, break it down and you're left with three main colours. Trio tip.

You might find something in a fantastic print that you can't ignore in the shop, bring it home and it will speak to an item you already have – they will have a conversation you weren't expecting – and the reason you know that is because of the way they will make you feel when you put them together. I get a feeling of excitement when something feels good on, I know instinctively that the two pieces are talking to each other – and if you start to listen to that feeling you get, you'll know it too. Often when I get that feeling, I want to share the outfit on social media because I know that I will have something valid to say about it – a way of discussing how the separates came to be a whole; how the colour or the texture made me feel. For me, I have to be able to say something when I post an image of myself – there has to be a reason for it.

LAYER UP

I have been called the 'layering queen' which is a big compliment because I am not entirely sure whether I am doing anything all that unique to be honest! It's a way I have always dressed and, actually, it probably stemmed more from feeling self-conscious about parts of myself and dressing to disguise them.

Back in the nineties, I was inspired by the likes of Courtney Love layering satin camisole dresses over band tee shirts, or tying a checked shirt around the waist of a smarter dress. Sometimes the item would disguise or distract from a part of my body that I didn't feel all that comfortable showing off, while other times it was a way of adding another colour or pattern into my outfit. Don't let the thought of school uniforms put you off playing around with layers. Just because you once wore tights, a vest, a shirt, a jumper *and* a coat doesn't mean you can't do the same now and make it fashion! It's also a highly effective dressing technique for women going through the menopause, when their internal body temperatures might go from 0 to 60 in a few seconds. Taking the time to work out exactly what pieces you need to layer can really help.

I have found that certain ways of dressing just work for me – and it follows the same principles. Sometimes I just don't want to bare my arms, so I'll layer a long-sleeved tee underneath a short-sleeved one. Occasionally I just want to inject an extra splash of colour into my outfit – or add in an extra print. Print and pattern make me feel more 'me'. I can do plain, but feel better when there's something else going on. Layering isn't just a great way of putting together a more unique look, it helps make the most of pieces that might just let gather dust in your wardrobe. Summer dresses that you love but just wouldn't wear in the middle of winter. Well no, on their own that might be a bit nippy, but could you layer a polo neck underneath and add a pair of tights and ankle boots?

I have been trying to work out how to explain layering in written form. I've done it for years – so often it is tricky actually writing down something you just *do*! The easiest thing is to take it right back to basics. Please remember these aren't hard-and-fast 'rules'; they're just styling tricks I person-ally like and have done while styling models and myself for years. One of my favourite ways to layer is to bring pieces together in a new way. Often, it's the juxtaposition of two or more very different items of clothing that make an outfit unique and more interesting – and if I were to offer any advice at all, it's to keep trying. Have fun with things – take out that conventional 'sense' of pairing certain pieces with others and see how it feels if you layered a blouse under a tee shirt, or an oversized knit cardigan over a silky slip dress.

An easy way to start is to take a piece most of us will own in one form or another: a Breton striped top. I own *quite* a few, from thin jersey to thicker cotton and I find I wear them all on rotation often, depending on what it is I am pairing them with. As an aside, if you don't already have them, I would definitely consider buying a couple of different colours of striped tops to have in your wardrobe. They may be an item you've previously avoided because you've followed the 'rule' about them making you appear wider. But striped tops are brilliantly useful multitaskers and there are so many styles available that you can always find one to flatter and fit your shape. You don't need to go for expensive versions either – some of the best layering pieces I own have come from H&M and Zara, but I also recommend Saint James for traditional mariner tops (thicker cotton) and ARKET for thin, tissue-weight pieces.

Keeping things simple, if you wear a lot of black to, say, the office, you might have a few plain, short-sleeved dresses you wear often. To help ring the changes, you could try layering a black-and-white, crew neck, striped long-sleeved tee underneath. Even if your dress has a high neckline, you're making it a bit more interesting with your stripy arms. You could then add a blazer over the whole look, push back the sleeves of the blazer and just give a little flash of stripe. If you wear dresses that have a V-neckline or are lower at the front, try playing around with proportion and wear a higher neck beneath, like a polo or turtleneck. This juxtaposition of different necklines will be interesting, but you're keeping the colours consistent with the monochrome stripes.

Personally, I treat stripes in the same way I do a leopard print and consider them two of my most useful mixing and layering prints. Often, I go to post an image of myself on Instagram wearing another jumper or dress layered over a stripe and worry that I have done it before. But actually, what I should be thinking is, 'This works for me and, yep, here I am doing it again!' Find that signature style! Another regular feature I try to show on social media is a few ways to wear one piece – and for me, it's always way more interesting to show how pieces can work in a non-traditional way by layering, or recalibrating the way I see them.

Case in point, recently I styled a dress from a high-street store. It was, for me, the perfect kind of dress with which to multitask, in that it was a button-up-front shirt style. I would say the shirt dress – either knee-length or midi – is one of the most useful pieces, because of the many ways you can style it. You don't just need to look at it as a dress. This one was midi-length, had a navy blue base colour (classic) and a bold, painterly splash print of various colours including ochre, rust, khaki green and white. Those tertiary shades are ones

I naturally gravitate towards and the whole colour combination definitely inspired me to put together looks that weren't restricted to wearing the dress on its own – as pretty as it was, it just was a little bit staid.

Always take a second to assess how a piece makes you feel. While I didn't *love* the dress on its own, I loved how inspired it made me feel – I really wanted to try to style it in different ways to create several looks. First off, I removed the belt that came with it. As I have already mentioned, I am not a huge fan of a standard matching belt. I considered the dress initially as a long-line blouse, so buttoned it down to the waist and then left the buttons on the bottom half undone. Taking a skirt that I already owned, in the same rust colour as the print on the dress, I put that on underneath – so the dress was over the top of the skirt. There were quite a few options I considered for accessories, but I loved the idea of pulling in another colour from the print of the dress.

I found a khaki cotton sash belt from a raincoat and tied that around my waist which gave a little nod to another colour from the dress. Because I was sticking to pieces that took their lead from the colours in the dress's print, the outfit pulled together as the eye connects up all the same colours. By the way, this also works on a tonal sliding scale, so rather than the rust, a deeper, more burgundy version of it could also work. Or rather than the khaki green, you could try a paler, minty green. Treating the dress as a blouse gave me the confidence to layer it over another separate – in this case a skirt – but a shirt dress also works over trousers in the same way, i.e. buttoned to the waist and left undone, worn as a tunic or blouse.

For another look with the same dress, I put a pair of white jeans beneath (picking up my cue from the white in the print), worn with a favourite navy-and-white striped polo neck (a classic go-to). The navy and white is in the dress print and so the pattern clash works (your eye connects the two colours). I layered over the dress, did up a few of the buttons from the chest down and added a chunky pair of navy-and-white tweed sandals, which gave the whole look a bit more of an edge. Obviously, it does all come down to personal taste and there's no right or wrong here – so if you wanted to wear this with plimsolls or even lace-up brogues, you absolutely could. If you wanted to, you could further layer this by leaving all of the buttons of the dress undone – so it's worn more like a kimono – and adding in a longline sleeveless jacket in a contrasting navy texture, for example, a wool mix or sheepskin.

I also tried the dress with a terracotta plain cotton polo neck beneath, worn with black satin wide-leg trousers in a cropped ankle length. Black and navy *do* work together, no matter what previous rules state! If it's good enough for perennially chic women such as French *Vogue*'s Emmanuelle Alt or Carine Roitfeld, it's definitely good enough for the rest of us! Plus, black and navy aren't so different in terms of their colour density, so there isn't too strong a contrast.

Finally, for this outfit, I added an ochre-coloured trench coat over the top, to pick out the ochre from the splashes within the print. It meant I had kept two pieces of my layering (the polo neck and the trench) to the exact colours within the print, while the final item – my trousers – were black and therefore dark enough to ground the look and pull everything together. (All the images are on my Instagram if you fancy scrolling back to see how they looked together!)

Fabric choice plays a big role when you layer – it really does make a difference. The satin trousers were lightweight and matched the weight of the dress, meaning I wasn't trying to pair a heavy tuxedo-style trouser with a lightweight dress fabric, which would have thrown off the proportion. They also had an elasticated waist and were slightly cropped, so they felt informal. Consider the weights of the separates you're trying to layer and, where possible, keep things similar for balance.

Texture is also a really interesting way of layering pieces together. For example, you could stick to an entirely tonal colour palette of beige and white, but if you add in contrasting textures together it makes for a much more interesting overall look. Start off with a pair of white or cream wide-leg jeans, as an example. On your top half add a long-sleeved white tee, then layer with a cream Aran knit or cable knit, embellished with beads, and push up the sleeves so you see a hint of the white tee beneath. Over the top of that you could add a buttonless, collarless, edge-to-edge wool boyfriend coat in a cream-and-beige check and *then* add a beige sheepskin waist-length gilet over the top of the coat.

The collarless and buttonless aspect of the coat keeps things simple – there's a lot going on and you're really aiming for more of a streamlined look to allow the texture of the jumper to be the hero. Finish off with a brown leather bag and/or boots (or white trainers) and while you've kept the colours similar throughout, you've also brought in a lot of interest visually with all the various textures. It's a very simple way to create a look filled with personality without shouting about it in loud prints.

You can also layer knitwear in an interesting way, by draping a contrast or tonal jumper over your shoulders, while wearing another. It's this slightly contradictory element that adds a quirk to your outfit – also, it's always been considered chic to throw a jumper around your shoulders! Push that contradictory element as far as your nerve allows. You could start off by pairing informal with more formal; layering a slouchy grey marl sweatshirt with a tulle maxi skirt, for example. Or if the thought of that terrifies/horrifies you, try wearing a knitted hoody underneath a smart, structured coat. You could get more wear out of your favourite summer skirt if you wear it with a long-sleeved tee, under a vintage band tee and throw a cardigan over the top. Or dress down that occasion dress you spent a fortune on but rarely have the opportunity to wear by layering a cashmere crew neck *over* the top of it, effectively reconfiguring it as a skirt.

In fact, layering in the way of that last example is an excellent way of reappraising those pieces that tend to just hang in your wardrobe but are rarely worn. Fashion should be fun – you should be able to wear and repeat-wear favourite pieces in new ways. Don't save them for best, just reinvent them with other pieces. Sequins shouldn't just be for holidays or late-night parties – work the contrast and pair them with a sweatshirt or jeans, trainers and an oversized coat. Invest in pieces you know you're going to be able to use in this way. I bought a khaki shacket (shirt/jacket) about 10 years ago from Topshop, but it's been with me on every holiday. It's the piece I wear while on the aeroplane, layered over a tee or a cashmere jumper *and* used as a cover up on cooler evenings in the sunshine. It's cotton, so gets softer and more loved with every wash! (I also have a cotton dressing gown that my brother brought back from a Japanese hotel room which has travelled the world with me!) These pieces are precious – they tell your stories, they've shared the special times. Look after them and give them more love, just try to vary the ways.

As I mentioned earlier, layering is also a great technique to try if you struggle with body temperature – women going through the menopause is a classic example. I have a very stylish friend who always wears layers for that very reason – and while she's made it her mission to find pieces that look great, they're actually there for a very simple reason: she doesn't want to overheat. Her layering superheroes are a pair of footless tights – she would rather have leggings and then wear thinner pop socks in her shoes – a loose fit dress, usually with a V-neckline, usually in a print, and then a contrast print long-sleeved cotton top underneath. She has a large bust, so feels the proportion of having a V-neckline on the dress, combined with the focus of a print detail from the long-sleeved tee shirt just beneath her chin, is more flattering for her shape.

DEVELOPING YOUR STYLE

It's interesting to me that people say style is something you're born with. I don't necessarily think that's true. As I mentioned earlier, style – and specifically shopping for your style – is something you can definitely 'learn'. You can practise 'style', consider the pieces you feel good in and remind yourself of them as you put others together. You can take your time, in your own time, practising and experimenting with your wardrobe combinations. Setting that time aside every now and then helps you see your clothes with a fresh pair of eyes – and taking inspiration from other areas of your life may allow you to consider new combinations, or pieces you might need.

There is instinct involved in this skill, but finding your sense of style is something that can definitely be developed, particularly when you start to take notice of the way others dress. Never be afraid to stop a stranger on the street, say how lovely they look and ask where something you've admired has come from. Or just tell them you think they look great. Nothing – and I mean nothing – is guaranteed to put a smile on your face as much as a stranger taking time out to say they like your vibe! Look at the way people whose sense of style you admire combine colour or separates and take your cue from them. I did it myself. Straight after university I landed work experience in the fashion department of a BBC morning TV show. On my first day, I remember being absolutely terrified about what on earth I should wear. You have to bear in mind that at this point, my fashion experience was minimal. I'd left university and only had a babysitting-earnings budget for the odd Topshop piece. My interning wardrobe was mainly made up of clothes I wore to lectures. Mum bought me a couple of items she considered 'work-appropriate', but Mum was an office manager for a large multinational company, not a fashion editor, and our visions about appropriate work garments weren't really on the same page!

I had wanted to be a fashion journalist from the age of nine. But university newspaper articles aside, my style training was my, frankly, obsessive interest in fashion magazines, combined with the knowledge that I could put outfits together – my friends' reactions told me that. Crucially, I was desperate to learn. As the *very* junior assistant to the assistant on the styling team, all of my money was going on travel (I had moved down south from the north-west of England to live with my aunt and uncle), not clothes. So, I played it safe – I did what I believed every fashion assistant had to do, and wore black, from head to toe. To be fair, I had a point – black is one of those colours that always tends to look expensive, regardless of where you buy your pieces from, be it Prada or Primark. All the while, like a sponge, I soaked up *everything* the stylists on the show discussed, dissected (in my head!) the way they put outfits together and the pieces they told each other about.

I remember one of the team's stylists talking about a particular pair of embroidered slippers you could only get from a couple of stores in Chinatown, and about how she had taken them to a cobbler's, who added a sturdier sole to them and she started wearing them with jeans and a tee. They added a bit of her personality to a very simple, everyday look. Another was obsessed with vintage clothes' markets and took me out with her to help as she discovered niche stalls in London's Notting Hill – or rummaged around slightly more upmarket shops in Covent Garden selling pre-loved designer gear. She taught me how to shop for vintage, showing me the pieces that never date and how a second-hand coat won't just look great, but will also help create your own style.

The way the team analysed outfits, debated why certain things were 'cool' and why others didn't work was all revelatory to my mind. I deduced that, actually, it didn't matter where pieces came from – but it did matter how they made you feel. It's not about where you shop; it's more about the importance you attach to each piece that comes into your life. Is it there as a good friend to stay forever or is it a fun-time Frankie? We all have different budgets and place importance on different levels of accessibility, so it's really about discovering those pieces that you instantly love, wherever you find them, and then putting them together in ways that give you those internal butterflies.

FIVE POINTS TO TAKE AWAY

1. Sizes and numbers don't really matter, but if you want an outfit to have balance and power, proportions do.

2. You are the only fashion authority you need to listen to. You can appreciate the ideas of others, but your gut instinct and response to clothes is all you need.

3. Working out the proportions that best work for you will make shopping *and* dressing easier. You'll have a greater understanding of the shapes to buy to wear with your existing clothes and also those that would make great investments.

4. If you fancy trying print or colour, but aren't sure where to start, think about your outfit content in terms of three. The predominant colour is the focus, then add a print or block taken from that predominant colour as well as an accent colour.

5. Always take a second to assess how a piece makes you feel. If you get a feeling of excitement when you put something on, that's how you know a piece works for you.

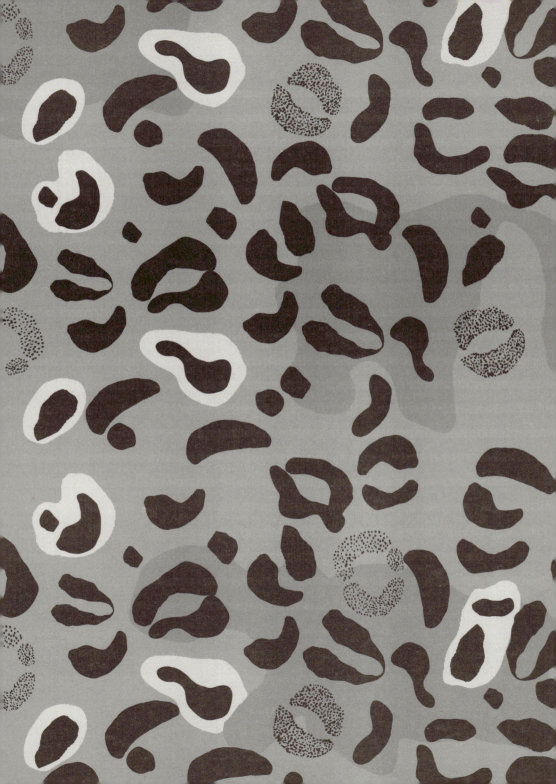

Why Your Age No Longer Matters

CHAPTER EIGHT

WHY YOUR AGE NO LONGER MATTERS

Fashion you can buy, but style you possess. The key to style is learning who you are, which takes years. There's no how-to road map to style. It's about self-expression and, above all, attitude.

—Iris Apfel

I am in my early forties. It's ridiculous really, because in my head I'm still around 24. My mum said something to me once, when I was in my early teens, and it's stuck with me ever since. As she was putting make-up on in the bathroom – and I stood there watching, probably being annoying and asking if I could have a perm or my ears pierced – she looked at herself in the mirror and said, 'It's funny, you never feel any different inside, then you look at yourself and get a shock.' I smiled and dismissed her words, without really comprehending or understanding. But they stuck somewhere inside my head, only to be retrieved decades later, when I too looked in the mirror – and got a shock.

I spot little changes in the mirror myself and wonder what's happening. I feel a change. I feel 'in-between'. Without make-up, I look tired, not fresh-faced. My hair doesn't do its thing anymore. Where once I could spritz and leave, now I can't leave it to dry naturally – I have to *do* it. The greys sprout aggressively from the top of my head, so I can't do that fashionable balayage thing. I look in the mirror now and see lines that weren't there before, while the next minute, teenage-style spots appear on my chin, hormonal and angry (much like an actual teenager!). And don't get me started on the random *chin hairs* that pop up out of nowhere. I have to carry a pair of tweezers wherever I go, because who knows when they will strike?

It is an odd feeling, seeing the 'you' you know disappear a little. Every couple of months, I have an inch cut from the bottom of my hair and have bleach slathered on my going-grey, frizzier-than-before roots. I also get my eyebrows threaded every month. I'm not super high-maintenance, but it's a bit of regular self-care that makes me feel better about myself. I definitely can't drink alcohol in the same way I used to, not if I want a proper night's sleep and a slightly flatter stomach! Some days I just want a grown-up to sort everything out – then I realise I *am* the grown-up! I have discovered the joy of a double cleanse in the evening and a retinol application before bed. I now use an eye cream, I

slather on hand lotion and *always* make sure my face mois-
turiser extends down to my chest. I haven't had Botox or any
kind of filler yet, but never say never. You have to do what's
right for you, no judgement here.

But it's true, ageing *is* a privilege. A good friend died last
year, something that we all sadly experience at some point in
our lives. She was 45 and it was way too soon. Her nine-
year-old son and husband lost the most wonderful woman
and *none* of it seems fair. So, I do not talk about these physical changes with any kind of negativity. In fact, bring it on.
It can all be sorted. The grey hairs don't matter – they can
be dyed if you want. The rogue chin upholstery? That can be
plucked, epilated, waxed or tweezed. The extra padding around
the middle that seems to just arrive and then, like a guest
outstaying her welcome, just doesn't seem to leave? It doesn't
really matter. No one is looking at you sideways on the train.
There is a confidence that comes with having lived. Even
though the external 'us' is starting to change, the inside of us
hasn't. All the things that make us tick and productive and
happy haven't changed. I know exactly who I am and what
it is I can offer. I can say 'no' easily, without worrying about
trying to please. I don't care so much. Not in a callous way,
but one that allows me to say, 'No thank you' or 'That actually
doesn't work for me', rather than saying yes – as I have done
in the past – and for it to end up being a chore. We've had

careers, families – biological or chosen; we've failed and we've succeeded. I'm much happier in this skin than the more youthful version of it, because now I know who I am.

Ageing *should* be respected, we *should* respect our elders, but the fashion boundaries that have previously existed between the generations have blurred – now it's all about an ageless style. My grandmother, Evangeline, died when I was 26. She was a huge part of my life and a *very* strong character. At this point, I'd love to be able to share how she was the most stylish woman I've ever met and passed down her love of fashion – along with her Chanel 2.55 handbag – but alas, no. She had very little interest in fashion! She dressed in the typical 'woman of a certain age' way that you just don't see so much of these days. (She didn't much like food either. Or the colour lilac, or going out all that often. She liked to get home so she could 'stroke the walls'. She was, as they say, a character!) Her uniform was a pair of slacks – brown or navy – worn with a little polyester knitted crew neck in a variety of colours, bought from Littlewoods or Marks & Spencer. Or if she was going out, she would wear a pleated midi skirt, a pussy bow blouse and a hand-knitted cardigan – for she was a prodigious knitter before her hands were crippled by arthritis.

My mother, who was her daughter-in-law, bought Grandma a purple and yellow silky two-piece for her golden wedding anniversary party which she was thrilled with – it was the first time Mum had ever seen her excited by clothes! She just wasn't very interested. The reason I am bringing her up is because my *own* mum is the grandma now – and there is a whole *world* of difference with how she dresses compared to the way my grandmother did, just one generation later. There are 26 years between Mum and me, we live in different parts of the country and have very different shapes, but have both unknowingly bought exactly the same piece from the same shop. She's often called me excitedly to say she has just bought something I've worn and shared on Instagram because she loved it too. Because, while we might wear things differently, those lines are blurred. There is no longer a fixed generational mindset when it comes to the stores we 'have to shop in'.

AGE IS JUST A NUMBER

If you think about it, we're a generation that's, actually, almost ageless. We have rejected the old-fashioned notions that women over 40 have to look and act a certain way. They may still exist, but you can choose to ignore the age-shaming, unsolicited advice from editorials in magazines sharing 'rules' about dressing and age. In fact, *please do* ignore it. 'A bob at this stage could put a decade on you!' 'Don't wear a miniskirt or flash too much cleavage if you don't want to look like mutton dressed as lamb!' It's all rubbish. Why should we have to start showing restraint? Or worse, hide. 'Put down those jeans or leather leggings, you need to opt for classic slacks now!' 'For God's sake don't show any skin!' 'Cut your hair!' 'Wear beige!' 'Occupy less space!' 'Don't draw attention to yourself!' . . . I mentioned the parallel earlier, but imagine a men's magazine suggesting a man of a certain age put on a polo neck to disguise his jowls or neck wrinkles.

Nobody feels any different inside, so why are we adhering to advice that suggests we have to down tools once we spot that first wrinkle? It's kind of ridiculous – and we've been sold a pup for too long! What it really comes down to is the fact that we should never stop learning. I wouldn't consider that I know absolutely everything at my age, so must immediately stop listening to any new information, so why would I consider I know everything there is to know about my style? It's an incredibly personal evolution. It ebbs and flows with weight gain, loss, sickness, health, events or lifestyle changes. It's not about putting the brakes on and hitting the emergency stop at a sartorial place deemed socially accept-able, just because we've arrived at a certain age. Now is the time we *can* accelerate. We can always try things out, take risks, have fun; we're just hitting our stride. You might be tuned into the pieces you like, and that's great, but you're never too old to give something a new twist. That rule about never wearing something you remember from the first time around? Also rubbish. You understand the shapes and colours you're attracted to, so never stop experimenting.

Our role models are different. We have incredible women in the public eye who are intelligent, successful, beautiful and proud of themselves *and* their age. We no longer need to look to youth as the benchmark of beauty – because it's so blindingly obvious there's a whole roster of women past the age of 40 who are *just getting going.* Helen Mirren, Zadie Smith, Vera Wang, Michelle Obama, Jane Fonda, Oprah Winfrey, Meryl Streep, Nigella Lawson, J.K. Rowling, Pat McGrath, Kimberley Motley, Sheryl Sandberg, Arundhati Roy – I mean, do I need to go on?

Lauren Hutton appeared on the cover of a magazine I read recently – a beautiful close-up portrait of her almost-80-year-old face, writ large with her life lived; wrinkles, lines, sparkling eyes, gorgeous, gap-toothed smile. She took my breath away with her *real* beauty – and it made me consider how much *unreality* we accept as normal. It's about visibility. It's about seeing accomplished role models out there, in the public eye. It's not about accepting being written off as soon as the grey hairs set in. It's about allowing our children to see these incredible women and showing that age is not something to hide or be feared. We need to see more of the reality. We need to read less about how great they are 'for their age'.

To be honest, we owe it to our children to keep pushing back on these societal age agendas. Of course, we know this already. We know intellectually that we shouldn't need to look a certain way or be a certain age to avoid being pigeon-holed or stereotyped. We understand that sexuality can be complex, multifaceted and indelibly part of who we are. And yet . . . And yet . . . So, I will say it regardless. We owe our daughters the chance to be judged by their brains and their actions, rather than their hair or their dress size. They deserve to know that their *choice* in dress doesn't mean *anything*, other than it's how *they* have chosen to be seen. Grey hair and wrinkles *will* happen to all of us – and that simple, unalterable fact needs to be normalised, without them learning the sense that society wants us to cover them up. That our children won't feel a pressure to cover up and hide away as soon as they hit 40, 50, 60-plus – and that, actually, it's a majestic time of life! The things we know! The wisdom we can share! The f*cks we no longer have to give! We owe our sons the uncensored truth: that women bleed every month, it's no biggie, but it can be uncomfortable and it might make them emotional; that buying sanitary products for your mum/sister/partner/mate isn't embarrassing – it's considerate. And here's one – that sex doesn't look *anything* like it does on the porn sites they might start to look at. Sex isn't something that's 'done' to women; it's a mutually desired, brilliant experience. Be safe, have fun; it should make you feel great – and if it doesn't, that's an issue. That women, when naked, all look a little bit different, but guess what? Pubic hair is normal!

Male film stars are still cast as action heroes or lovers well into their fifties and beyond, while females become the 'mother' or the 'family friend' or the 'widow'. Slowly things are changing – we are seeing more representative women up there on our screens, with female actors including Reese Witherspoon, Charlize Theron, Lena Waithe, Margot Robbie, Issa Rae, Sandra Bullock and Kerry Washington all setting up their own production companies specifically to get female-centric stories about women of all ages turned into TV shows and films – because, 'Hi, we're here! It's not all about the way we look!'

For *so* long, advertising has relied on youth in order to shift products. Specifically, over the past couple of years, brands have been relying on a well-known set of Instagram-famous models, including Cindy Crawford's daughter Kaia Gerber, alongside reality star daughters, Gigi and Bella Hadid, as well as Kendall Jenner, to front their marketing campaigns in a bid to attract those important Millennial and Gen-Z customers. The problem is that while they create a buzz, many of those models have an overlapping audience and their reach only goes so far in terms of encouraging spend. For such a long time, the fashion industry has ignored the fact that there is an *entire demographic* of women out there with disposable cash and a desire to look good. The Internet, however, has changed everything. This generation now has a voice. Social media has provided a platform for women of all ages to share, enjoy and showcase their own style – and it has *democratised* fashion. It allows women of all ages to say this is what we look like, this is what we wear, get *over* our ages, because this is who we are.

Take a cue from the stylish older ladies showcasing their fashion sense on social media. Be inspired by the likes of Renata Jazdzyk from @venswifestyle, a self-confessed 'ageism fighter' who produces editorial-style Insta images showing the latest designer it-pieces. Colleen Heidemann (@colleen_heidemann) is a former flight attendant turned vintage store owner and is the epitome of glamour, aged 70. Tennille Murphy aka the fabulous @thetennillelife_ posts about all things food, fitness, design and travel. Helen Van Winkle, aka @baddiewinkle on Instagram, posts images that are full to the brim with whimsy and sass, while Grece Ghanem (@greceghanem) is a Canadian personal-trainer-turned-fashion-influencer whose style code is inherently chic, but she's not afraid of more out-there trends either. Former stylist Linda Rodin (@lindaandwinks) once worked with stars including Madonna, before finding herself an unlikely It girl at the age of 65, while 60-something grandmother Lyn Slater created a flourishing social media account based around the accidental aspect of her influencer career: @iconaccidental. Lyn has started to change the conversation with the brands she works with and refuses to pigeon-hole herself, or her audience, once saying, 'I would rather pressure MAC Cosmetics to think of me as a consumer, than help promote a separate over-50 make-up brand'.

Actress and singer Jennifer Lopez, who turned 50 in 2019, is now the 'face' of fashion brand Versace – a full 360-degree move from them, 20 years after she wore their now-iconic jungle-print, slash-front dress to the Grammys. In fact, returning to Jennifer is something of a sure bet for Versace. According to global fashion search engine Lyst, after Jennifer closed the Spring/Summer 2020 Versace show wearing the same jungle-print dress, she 'broke the Internet', generating an estimated $9.4 million in media mentions and online engagement. Her Super Bowl 2020 half-time performance, alongside singer Shakira (who celebrated her forty-third birthday on stage), was a complete triumph and an example of two sexy, powerful women owning the stage – and for whom their ages are the least interesting thing about them.

Paying attention to this phenomenon is a no-brainer for brands, financially. The over-55s are set to be the fastest-growing demographic over the next five years, according to research by Mintel. They're a generation working later, or retiring from office work, only to presents some other kind of work for themselves. It presents a need for professional, stylish clothing until later in life, meaning that women who are style-conscious have money to spend on their busy lives. Which is why it's interesting that Versace have returned to Jennifer Lopez – because they see it too. Remember the furore when Isabella Rossellini was dumped as the face of Lancôme, just a few days past her forty-third birthday in 1990? At the time, she was the highest-earning model in the world, but her age was an issue. She has since said, 'While the marketing research people told me that women were responding to me, the client didn't seem to be happy that they had a woman in their forties representing their product. The executive at the time told me that advertising is about dreams. And the dream allegedly was that women dream to be young.' After her name was *still* mentioned in marketing research years later, Rossellini was asked by Lancôme's new *female* director if she'd return to the brand again, aged 63.

The same thing happened to Lauren Hutton, previously cast as 'the face' of Revlon in the seventies – demanding a contract that turned her into the highest paid model of the generation, earning $250,000 per year and changing the way the industry worked (brand ambassador roles and long-term contracts were used from then on). But when she turned 41, the brand cancelled their contract with Hutton. She has said, 'When they called me in to say it was goodbye, they told me they had done "focus groups" and discovered that "women over 40 didn't use make-up!" Well, I was over 40, and all the women I knew all used make-up.' Today, Lauren is the face of clinical skincare brand StriVectin, about whom she has said, 'The executives (mostly women) are smart enough to know that women over 40 have value and that women in their seventies are still vibrant and thriving. It's the new age of ageing. It's taken years to get here and I'm glad to be a part of it. I have always said that if my life could stand for one thing, it would be to change the way women feel about getting older.'

There are – as mentioned earlier – *plenty* of sites catering to the young; Boohoo, ASOS, I Saw It First and In The Style are all targeting a very young market who want a Kardashian-ready Instagram look. Recently I had a conversation with a public relations friend in the industry and I was moaning about the fact that I used to find really great pieces on sites like ASOS, but struggle to find anything much beyond neon cycling shorts and crop tops these days. His response was simple: those brands are no longer interested in appealing to a 40-something woman. They want the young. And it's a funny place to be – when there's a subtle sense of being pushed out of the door by stores you previously felt so comfortable and accepted by. And you're left, confused, standing outside, wondering where it is you need to shop now. It's usually at this stage you might start considering the beige slacks and sensible shoes, but don't – because there's no need!

It's about finding stores and brands that speak to your personality, not your age. In a slightly off-tangent way, but bear with me, I have friends with high-profile social media accounts who were dropped from brand collaborations and social media fashion campaigns once they publicly announced their pregnancies. It was suggested the brands had to be careful being associated with them, as they didn't offer standard maternity wear and it would have been 'confusing' to their customers. Now personally, I didn't happen to wear a lot of maternity wear during my pregnancies – in fact, I tried to choose clothes that would work from my usual favourite stores and just bought a larger size. There were a few things that didn't work – trousers being one – but imagine a virtual Venn diagram of clothing and maternity wear, where there's a lovely overlap that *could* exist. Brands have the potential to expand on sales (and improve their sustainability) by catering within their mainline collection to pregnant women who may be able to buy 'that' dress in a larger size, offering petite, regular, tall and maternity versions of the same trousers or adding in oversized button-up shirts that would work for post-partum feeding too. It's the same with an older customer base; clothing ranges don't need to scream 'Here we are!' to a specific demographic, it's just that the party needs to include an invitation to everyone. We can all make up our own mind about what it is we want to wear – it'd just be nice to be able to party in the main room and not be forced to find what we can in the kitchen.

However, there are sites out there that actually start out responding to a niche within a cultural market, but find themselves a much wider audience because of the collections they buy.

For so long, we have all been led by style rules, but I think there is actually only one question to ask yourself when it comes to your clothes, regardless of your age: 'Does it make me happy?' If you feel happy in what you're wearing, you will radiate happiness to those around you and that's what dressing should be about. A good fashion investment isn't simply down to the *cost per wear*, but to the amount of *joy per wear* it will give you. It could be a beautiful leop-ard-print coat, or it could be a vintage dress you spotted and aren't sure where on earth you'll wear it, but it makes you feel fabulous. As I've previously mentioned, the 'saving it for best' mantra just shouldn't be in your vocabulary. It's the same as saying, 'I can't wear that at my age'. Everything can be worn, whenever you like – it's just a question of how.

THE PIECES THAT MAKE A DIFFERENCE

Wearing a colour near your face – and remember, the colour should make you look bright-eyed and bushy-tailed – will do wonders for your skin. My mum – at the age of 70 – feels very strongly that she now has to 'cover up' her neck and chest because of her age. And I think here it's a case of doing what makes you feel more comfortable. There are no rules about *having* to cover up, because guess what? We *all* age! Our bodies change – so there may be more lines or age spots, but don't feel you have to disguise that. If you do, look for ways of integrating an accessory like a scarf into your outfit, perhaps draped around your neck or worn a bit like a tie under a collar and knotted into a bow at the front. Or experiment with layering different tops – polo neck under V-neck, or camisole over turtleneck, until it's less about feeling the need to 'disguise' and more about creating your own vibe.

It's the same with a pair of statement earrings or a long necklace – ring the changes with accessories that can alter the mood of a dress. Wear trainers with it rather than heels – and add a leather biker jacket rather than a blazer. You don't have to look conservative just because you're over 40, 50 or beyond. You can – and should – still shine. Who is to say a leather jacket isn't precisely the kind of fashion rebel your organised wardrobe is crying out for? Don't ignore colours because *you* think they're the preserve of the young and petite. Think about white as an example – you might previously have considered it too stark, or too young. But try using it with layers and different textures: lace cardigans over spaghetti strap cotton dresses, vintage embroidered blouses worn with ankle-grazer white jeans and sandals. Wearing sheer fabrics is a playful way to add white to your look, particularly if you're worried about showing off skin, as this creates the illusion of doing that, without *actually showing off skin*! And don't be afraid to wear sparkle outside of festive periods. Shimmer lifts an outfit and will make a casual ensemble look sophisticated. Think about a sequin silver skirt worn with a cream crew neck and silver accessories, or even dressed down totally with a grey marl sweatshirt and plimsolls. Or try an embellished, bejewelled cardigan thrown over your shoulders while wearing jeans and a plain tee.

I love coats and always find them the most useful part of putting an outfit together. They can tie in colours or prints from your outfit in a way that makes immediate sense, or simply bring in another shade to break up a head-to-toe look.

Always keep your eyes peeled for a coat that will brighten the flattest of days, when you know that wearing it will give you that inner kick you need – simple, unstructured styles with a raglan sleeve that have a bold colour pop; classic boyfriend single-breasted knee-length styles in a glorious pastel shade – and lift your basic pieces. Look for vintage coats in colours you wouldn't find anywhere else, or shapes and styles that add a splash of personality to a simpler outfit. I love vintage kimonos, which definitely don't have to be confined to the bedroom – pair them with ankle-length chinos and a simple white tee. Fifties dress coats – covered in sequins or embroidery – are always a brilliant find. I once discovered the most incredible dress coat in a tiny vintage shop in Portland, Maine. It was midnight-blue velvet, lined in faux fur and covered in beautiful gem-encrusted silver stars. I wore it to weddings, parties, winter events, even over a striped tee shirt and with casual trousers, only for it to disappear in a house move, never to be found again. I still dream about that coat!

Wearing a bright colour from top to toe will give you an immediate presence when you walk into a room and is also a great way to bolster any lagging self-confidence. Think about a hot hue of pink or orange in a silky shirt, with matching wide-leg, pyjama-style bottoms – add a bold lipstick and a great pair of earrings and you're sorted, *and* comfortable. Comfort – as I have said before – is key. Don't suffer in stiletto heels for an event just because you've always done it, when you spend the rest of your life wearing trainers or flat boots. Try a pair of platform heels instead, which have a degree of comfort and practicality that stilettos can't offer. Or just wear flats! There is now a whole world of party flats, where embellishment, colour, sequins and texture abound – just on a flat shoe rather than a heel. In fact, online shopping destination MATCHESFASHION has them as a specific category called 'evening flats'. It's a totally subjective issue, but I – despite being a very average five foot five – don't have any problem with putting on a gorgeous pair of flat shoes, depending on what it is I am wearing. It wouldn't bother me in the slightest that I wasn't in heels, or whether other people thought I *should* be wearing heels. In fact, I am often happier in flats because I know I'll be comfortable. My go-to places for party flats would be ASOS, Tabitha Simmons, Jimmy Choo and Boden. Don't feel you have to conform to old-fashioned dress codes if the mood takes you to wear a pair of flats.

Age really is nothing but a number. We shouldn't feel the need to hide away or cover up just because we've hit a certain milestone. In fact, there should be joy in rejecting the notion of being rejected, of caring less about what people think – or suggest we 'should' wear or do. There may be a need to tweak the shades you wear, to best complement your softer, more delicate skin and hair colour, but there's absolutely no need to completely overhaul yourself. The ideas behind the clothes you love and want to wear won't have changed – they still represent you, your style and your personality. You're still you, just a more mature version. The one with more stories to tell.

FIVE POINTS TO TAKE AWAY

1. Ageing is a privilege. There is a confidence that comes with having lived. Even though the external 'us' is starting to change, the inside hasn't. All the things that make us tick and productive and happy haven't changed.

2. It's a new age of ageing. Old-fashioned notions that women over 40 have to look and act a certain way should be rejected.

3. Don't listen to the rule about never wearing something you remember from the first time around. Style is an incredibly personal evolution and we should never stop experimenting, even if it means wearing something from a few decades ago!

4. Be inspired by a new generation of social media pioneers showcasing their own personal style. They have democratised fashion, allowing women of all ages to say 'This is what we look like; this is what we wear; this is who we are.'

5. When it comes to your clothes, regardless of your age, ask, 'Does it make me happy?' If you feel happy in what you're wearing, you will radiate happiness to those around you – and that's what dressing should be about.

A FINAL THOUGHT

One of the loveliest things about being on social media is the immediate feedback you receive from the people following you. It's not something I had in my previous incarnation as a print journalist. There were phone calls, emails, but mainly letters. In fact, there were a few occasions when we had to get the police involved in letters we received. There was even a regular – a man who wrote to us while serving at Her Majesty's pleasure (i.e. prison!). It wasn't so much the prison aspect that we were slightly taken aback by, more the fact he enjoyed sending detailed pencil drawings of a certain part of his, erm, anatomy.

Anyway, I digress. Now this immediate feedback is both a blessing *and* a curse. Sometimes you just want to share something you've enjoyed wearing, putting together or creating without agenda. And while the majority of people following will have a positive response (presumably because they've bought into your sense of style and appreciate it, otherwise they would just unfollow), there are always a few who like to 'be honest' and let you know just how little it suits you.

I don't mind an honest appraisal on occasion. But actually, if a photo or outfit isn't to their taste, I do think people should scroll on by and not engage at all. It's amazing how many times I have been sent a message or a comment has been left saying, 'I'm just trying to help . . .' or, 'You shouldn't . . .' or, 'I'm just saying what I think.' There is a modern notion that you *have* to be honest, in a kind of, 'Well, I'm just giving my opinion' way. You don't need to though, at all. Thinking, 'Is it necessary? Is it useful? Is it kind?!' before writing anything is a good guide! Life is too short to try to argue with people who don't know you or who don't care enough to, well, *care* about the fact that their words might hurt you. Ignore and move on.

But having said all that, the main feeling I get from social media is the warm sense of community. In my case, those who respond positively and kindly definitely outnumber those negatives. And I've started talking about how feedback *can* be a positive. I receive lots of messages from people (which I screenshot to read again on a bad day!) telling me how much I have helped their confidence when it comes to dressing. Sometimes when I am overthinking a caption, or wondering whether I should post a photo of myself, I stop and consider these messages and think *that's* why I am here. It's the most wonderful feeling to have been told you've helped someone feel better, even in the smallest of ways. It's so important to regularly curate your feed to make sure that's what you're feeling.

And if you take anything from this book at all, it's that. That the smallest of things can make the biggest difference. That sometimes all it takes is a small tweak, or a different colour shade, or even a simple shift in the way you view yourself. Rather than look at what's 'wrong' with you, instead look at the great stuff you've got going on! Because you absolutely have. You don't *need* to listen or accept the feedback or opinion of others if it makes you feel awkward, uncomfortable or upset. If the voice in your head is happy with what you've put on and how you feel wearing it, that is honestly all that matters. Rules can be helpful and offer structure – but they can also leave you feeling as though you're not up to scratch or missing the mark. Rules can always be broken. *You* can break them. Create your own. Be yourself.

REFERENCES

CHAPTER ONE

Donaldson, A., Mar. 2016. The power of fashion. British Council. Retrieved from https://www.britishcouncil.org/research-policy-insight/insight-articles/power-fashion.

GlobalData, 16 May 2019. UK mobile retail spend will double in the next five years to reach £33.2bn. Retrieved from https://www.globaldata.com/uk-mobile-retail-spend-will-double-in-the-next-five-years-to-reach-33-2bn/.

Hall, J., 11 Jun. 2019. Amazon 'to take one in every five pounds spent online by 2024'. Prolific London. Retried from https://www.prolificlondon.co.uk/marketing-tech-news/martech-news/2019/06/amazon-take-one-every-five-pounds-spent-online-2024.

Jahshan, E., 24 Apr. 2019. Boohoo posts bumper full year sales & profits haul. *Retail Gazette*. Retrieved from https://www.retailgazette.co.uk/blog/2019/04/boohoo-full-year-sales-profits-surge/.

Media Marketing, 6 Feb. 2016. Instagram is the most influential social network in marketing. Retrieved from https://www.media-marketing.com/en/news/instagram-is-the-most-influential-social-network-in-marketing/.

Singer, O., 7 Oct. 2017. Words of Wisdom From Edward Enninful and Marc Jacobs. *Vogue.* Retrieved from www.vogue.co.uk/article/oxford-union-edward-enninful-marc-jacobs-quotes

Smithers, R., 11 Jul. 2019. Fast fashion: Britons to buy 50m 'throwaway outfits' this summer. The *Guardian.* Retrieved from https://www.theguardian.com/fashion/2019/jul/11/fast-fashion-britons-to-buy-50m-throwaway-outfits-this-summer.

Szajna-Hopgood, A., 11 Dec. 2019. Zara owner Inditex posts 12% rise in profit. *Retail Gazette.* Retrieved from https://www.retailgazette.co.uk/blog/2019/12/zara-owner-inditex-posts-12-rise-in-profit/.

CHAPTER THREE

Goethe, J. W. V. and Eastlake, C. L. [translator], 2015. *Theory of Colours.* CreateSpace.

Smithers, R., 6 Apr. 2017. Britons expected to send 235m items of clothing to landfill this spring. The *Guardian.* Retrieved from https://www.theguardian.com/environment/2017/apr/06/britons-expected-to-send-235m-items-of-clothing-to-landfill-this-spring.

Taylor, A. P., 28 Feb. 2017. Newton's color theory, ca. 1665. The *Scientist*. Retrieved from https://www.the-scientist.com/foundations/newtons-color-theory-ca-1665-31931?archived_content=9BmGYHLCH6vLGNdd9YzYFAqV8S3Xw3L5.

CHAPTER FIVE

Bailey, G., 7 Mar. 2018. Women reveal the most annoying clothing pains they go through to look 'good'. The *Mirror*. Retrieved from https://www.mirror.co.uk/news/uk-news/women-reveal-most-annoying-clothing-12144659.

Reportlinker, 2 Dec. 2019. The athleisure market size was valued at $155.2 billion in 2018 and is expected to reach $257.1 billion by 2026, registering a CAGR of 6.7% from 2019 to 2026. PR Newswire. Retrieved from https://www.prnewswire.com/news-releases/the-athleisure-market-size-was-valued-at-155-2-billion-in-2018-and-is-expected-to-reach-257-1-billion-by-2026--registering-a-cagr-of-6-7-from-2019-to-2026--300967335.html.

Sun reporter, 7 Mar. 2018. One in 10 women say taking off their bra at the end of the day is better than sex. The *Sun*. Retrieved from https://www.thesun.co.uk/news/5744965/one-in-10-women-say-taking-off-their-bra-at-the-end-of-the-day-is-better-than-sex/.

The story of SPANX: Company timeline. QVC. Retrieved from https://www.qvc.com/footers/fa/pdf/SpanxFacts.pdf.

CHAPTER SIX

Morley, K., 16 Aug. 2018. One in every five pounds spent with UK retailers is now online, figures show. The *Telegraph*. Retrieved from https://www.telegraph.co.uk/news/2018/08/16/one-every-five-pounds-spent-uk-retailers-now-online-figures/.

Simpson, E., 23 Oct. 2019. High street: How many UK shops have closed? BBC News. Retrieved from https://www.bbc.co.uk/news/business-49349703.

CHAPTER EIGHT

Deeley, R., 16 Jan. 2020. Why the fashion industry is betting big on Jennifer Lopez. The Business of Fashion. Retrieved from https://www.businessoffashion.com/articles/news-analysis/why-the-fashion-industry-is-betting-big-on-jennifer-lopez.

Leaper, C., 26 Jan. 2020. The £7000 It dress: How Jennifer Lopez's Grammys fashion moment is sparking a sell-out 20 years later. The *Telegraph*. Retrieved from https://www.telegraph.co.uk/fashion/people/7000-dress-jennifer-lopezs-grammys-fashion-moment-sparking-sell/.

Mintel Press Team, 19 Sep. 2016. London Fashion Week: Older fashionistas lead in demands for more stylish clothing. Retrieved from https://www.mintel.com/press-centre/fashion/london-fashion-week-older-fashionistas-lead-in-demands-for-more-stylish-clothing.

Thomson Reuters and Dinar Standard, 2016. State of the global Islamic economy report 2016/17. Centre for Excellence in Islamic Finance. Retrieved from https://ceif.iba.edu.pk/pdf/ThomsonReuters-stateoftheGlobalIslamicEconomyReport201617.pdf.

ACKNOWLEDGEMENTS

A huge thank you to my literary agent, Lauren Gardner. Thanks for believing I could do it. To Lauren Whelan, my very patient editor at Yellow Kite, who has answered my many, many calls, emails and questions with so much kindness and consideration – and never so much as an eye-roll! To the rest of the Hodder crew – Eleni Lawrence, Caitriona Horne, Holly Whitaker, Sarah Christie and Julia Kellaway – thank you all for your enthusiasm, and your collective eyes and brains. It's been a joy working with you!

To Lucy Owen, my work rock and even lovelier pal, thank you for, well, everything. I couldn't do any of this without your tenacity, kindness and unwavering common sense. And to Sarah Pylas, who makes my working life so much easier and is just an absolute joy to have in it. Top Team! I am very grateful for you both.

Thank you to my husband, James, himself an ex-journo, who completely understood when I went into 'the zone' for weeks on end, shut the door and refused to speak to anyone! At least I think he did! To my children, Charlie and Lila, I love you and am so proud of you both. It's a strange new world I inhabit and I am so grateful to the three of you for supporting everything I do – and for only occasionally telling me to stop typing!

To my mum, Jenny, and dad, Alan, thank you for teaching me that you can achieve whatever it is you put your mind to – and for always being my biggest cheerleaders. I love you both. Thank you to my wonderful in-laws, John and Elizabeth, who couldn't be more supportive of us all. And to Stephen, Gareth, Liz, Joshua and Grace.

I've worked with some incredible women throughout my career – women who have inspired and supported me and continue to do so. When you find the good ones and you're lucky enough to work with them every day, hang on to them. Huge thanks to Trinny Woodall, not only for writing the foreword, but for being the best colour/print clash style inspiration there is. Special thanks to Jane Galpin for giving me my very first leg up on the ladder, to Sam Carlisle for taking a punt on hiring a *very green* 24-year-old all those years ago and to Jane Johnson for the most supportive words I could have heard after returning post-mat leave. That's the stuff that stays with you.

To my friends, who were there, encouraging and supporting, when I first mooted the idea of setting up a blog almost nine years ago. To Jeannie, my best friend from the age of four.

To all the friends I've made at work along the way, especially those on my teams at the *Mirror*, the *Sun* and *LOOK* – and to those who've become proper friends-from-the-'gram IRL too. I started listing you all, but I couldn't risk missing anyone out! To my gorgeous PR friends, who stuck around when I went freelance and who continue to do so. To *all* my friends – you know who you are. Thanks for being wonderful and always getting it, or at least pretending to.

When I was first approached with the idea of writing a book, I was overwhelmed with the very thought of it. But every message, email and DM I have received over the past eight and a bit years on social media asking for my advice has given me the confidence to finally do it. So, this acknowledgement list would be incomplete without the most enormous thank you to the wonderful tribe who follow me. Without you all this book *genuinely* wouldn't exist. Thank you for every message, comment, question, each DM that has ever started with, 'I saw this and thought of you . . .' and for every virtual conversation we've ever had. I appreciate every single one. It often feels like a very special place – and for that I say, thank you.

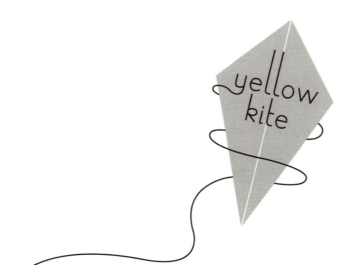

books to help you live a good life

Join the conversation and tell
us how you live a #goodlife

🐦 @yellowkitebooks
📘 YellowKiteBooks
📌 Yellow Kite Books
📷 YellowKiteBooks